# Participant Book
### For small-group study

## Adam Hamilton

Abingdon Press
*Nashville*

WHEN CHRISTIANS GET IT WRONG
PARTICIPANT BOOK

Copyright © 2010 by Abingdon Press

Scripture quotations in this publication, unless otherwise indicated, are from the New Revised Standard Version of the Bible, copyrighted © 1989 by the Division of Christian Education of the National Council of the Churches of Christ in the United States of America, and are used by permission.

Scripture quotations noted (NIV) are from the Holy Bible, NEW INTERNA-TIONAL VERSION®. Copyright © 1973, 1978, 1984 by International Bible Society. All rights reserved throughout the world. Used by permission of International Bible Society.

Scripture quotations noted (TNIV) are from the Holy Bible, TODAY'S NEW IN-TERNATIONAL VERSION®. Copyright © 2001, 2005 International Bible Society. All rights reserved. throughout the world. Used by permission of the International Bible Society.

Printed excerpts from Adam's interview with David Kinnaman are from an interview filmed in 2008, which is used by permission from the Barna Group.

This book is printed on acid-free, elemental chlorine-free paper.

ISBN 978-1-4267-1219-7

11 12 13 14 15 16 17 18 19—10 9 8 7 6 5 4 3

Manufactured in the United States of America

# CONTENTS

Introduction . . . . . . . . . . . . . . . . . . . . . . . . . . . 5

1. When Christians Are Unchristian . . . . . . . 9

2. Christians, Science, and Politics . . . . . . . . 23

3. When Speaking of Other Religions . . . . . 41

4. When Bad Things Happen . . . . . . . . . . . 57

5. In Dealing With Homosexuality . . . . . . . . 79

6. When Christians Get It Right . . . . . . . . . . 95

Postscript . . . . . . . . . . . . . . . . . . . . . . . . . . . 109

# INTRODUCTION

This guide is based on the book *When Christians Get It Wrong* (Abingdon Press, 2010). With the same topics and content included, this guide has added Scripture, discussion points, and examples to help small groups think, study, and discuss how Christians get it wrong and how we can begin to get it right.

For several years I have observed a growing frustration and sometimes open hostility toward Christianity on the part of an increasing number of people, particularly young adults. Even as a Christian pastor, I have found myself sometimes frustrated, embarrassed, or angry with expressions of Christianity that seem a far cry from the spirit of Jesus. I resonated with a woman who, after an encounter with a particular Christian, sent me an e-mail that said, "I no longer wish to call myself a Christian. I am still a follower of Jesus, but I see so many Christians who irritate me; and all I want to say is, 'I'm not one of them!' "

This is not entirely new. Gandhi spoke for many when he told Christian missionary E. Stanley Jones, "I love your Christ. It's just that so many of your Christians are so unlike your Christ."[1] Though there have been those in each generation who have felt this way, there is an increasing trend in this direction among young adults today.

In their 2007 book *unChristian*, David Kinnaman and Gabe Lyons outlined the research of the Barna Institute with hundreds of young adults who were outside the Christian faith. They found that 40% of all young adults (ages 16-29) have turned away from Christianity—more than in years past. Half of them consider themselves atheists or agnostics. The rest are spiritual, but they are not interested in Christianity or the church. Some of them even grew up in the church. It is not that they simply went away to college and decided to take a break from church for a few years. These young adults not only dropped out of church; they actually *rejected* the Christian faith.

Rather than exploring the theological issues that have turned these young people away from the Christian faith, the Barna Institute focused on understanding the perceptions they have of Christians. Their findings: 91% of those young adults surveyed who were outside the Christian faith felt Christians were "anti-homosexual"; 87% felt Christians were judgmental; 85% felt they were hypocritical; 75% felt they were too political; and 70% thought Christians were insensitive.

My conversations with young adults substantiate these findings. A few years ago our church set up a website to invite young adults (those under 35 by our definition) to tell us where they believe Christians get it wrong. About that same time we began sitting down to talk with others who had opted out of church. There were so many common responses. Generally I found that young people rejected Christianity not necessarily because of beliefs, although sometimes this was the case, but more often because of the attitudes and actions of Christians they have known or observed. Their criticism usually fell along one or more of several key themes:

- the unchristian ways some Christians act
- questions related to the role of God in human suffering and what Christians say to those who are suffering

- Christians' views of people of other world religions
- the anti-intellectual, anti-science stance of some Christians
- the politics of Christians
- the way Christians deal with homosexuality

My purpose in this book is for us to learn something from these young adults about the ways we get it wrong so that we may strive to get it right—to be the kind of Christians who draw people to Christ rather than push them away. We need to show the world a Christianity that helps them to see who Jesus really is. To do this, we will explore the key themes listed above with a specific focus on how we Christians can be more like Jesus as we relate and communicate to those who do not share our beliefs, particularly those outside the Christian faith. Then, in a concluding chapter, we will consider how returning to the basic or core teachings of Jesus can make us more effective in helping to bring about spiritual transformation in people's lives.

> ## What Did Jesus Say?
>
> *Love God and love your neighbor.*
> (Matthew 22:36-39; Mark 12:28-31; Luke 10:25-37)
>
> *Love your enemies.*
> (Luke 6:27-36; Matthew 5:43-48)
>
> *Others will know you are my disciples by your love for one another.*
> (John 13:34-35)

To make it a worthwhile journey that bears fruit in your life and witness, I invite you to be willing to let go of your biases and to question your assumptions. You will agree with some points and disagree with others. But as you are willing to view Christianity, the church, and even yourself from the perspective of those who are unimpressed with or even hostile to Christianity, you will come to discover how you may be a more influential representative of Christ in a skeptical world.

# 1

# WHEN CHRISTIANS ARE UNCHRISTIAN

*Now all the tax collectors and sinners were coming
near to listen to him. And the Pharisees and the
scribes were grumbling and saying, "This fellow
welcomes sinners and eats with them."*

(Luke 15:1-2)

A couple of years ago I had the opportunity to interview David Kinnaman, co-author with Gabe Lyons of the
2007 book *unChristian*. When I asked him to summarize
the findings presented in the book, this is what he said:

Young people are more secular than ever before. . . .
About one in five . . . are either atheist or agnostic
or [have] no faith. That compares to about one in
every twenty people . . . over the age of 60. Essentially, people believe Christianity is no longer like
Jesus intended. That's why they say it is unchristian. They believe essentially that we're hypocritical . . . judgmental . . . sheltered . . . too political . . .
anti-homosexual . . . too focused on getting con-
verts—that we're proselytizers. This negative set of

perceptions overwhelms any favorable ideas about seeing us doing good deeds [in] the world. They see this overwhelmingly negative picture of the church, and they reject Jesus and the church because they don't want to be associated with that kind of people.

If these words accurately describe how young adults have experienced Christians, is it any surprise that they are turning away from the Christian faith in droves?

When I've asked non-Christians what they think Jesus stood for, most say, "Love." And they are correct—this is one of the defining elements of Jesus' teaching. He told his followers that God's will for humanity could be summarized with two commands: love God and love your neighbor. He went on to say that our neighbor is anyone who needs our help. The love we are to show is not a feeling but a way of acting—kindness and compassion and a desire to bless and seek good for others. He told his disciples they were to love not only their neighbors and friends, but their enemies as well. He told them that the world would know that they are his disciples by their love. Most non-Christians know that Jesus stood for love, which is why it feels particularly off-putting when those who claim to follow Jesus act in unloving ways.

This disparity between the love Christians are meant to display and what young adults often experience is most pronounced when Christians speak with judgment or in disparaging ways toward others.

One young man described his experience when he was invited to attend a special youth group event at a big church in his town. He noted the kids rarely spoke to him at school until it was "bring a friend day" at youth group. They invited him to join their group at the local waterpark.

Here's his description of how the day went:

> It didn't start off badly; the rides at the park were fun, and I even enjoyed hanging out with some of them. But during the long ride back to the church, they started talking about people. They discussed who was having sex, who was smoking weed, who was gay. The more they talked, the worse things they said. Many of the people they were talking about were my friends, and they knew it! To make things worse, some of the ones talking loudest were doing the very things they were gossiping about. Finally, they got on to the subject of who was going to hell. It seems that if you didn't go to their brand of church, you didn't stand a chance of getting into heaven. That, of course, meant me, and it didn't seem to matter to them at all that I was sitting right there, soaking all this up.

The judgmentalism, hypocrisy, and unloving spirit these Christians displayed left this young man determined not to go back to church.

Another young woman echoed these same sentiments when she said,

> I'm thinking of the Christians in my school that I see every day. They judge everyone constantly. It's annoying and a lot of people don't really like it or like them because of it. I have a really good friend who claims to be a really hard-core Christian but he smokes weed all the time and drinks and does all these things and lies, and he's just not a Christian at all.

Both of these young people turned away from the Christian faith because of the actions of young Christians they knew. But this is not a phenomenon that is unique to young people. No doubt you can think of your own example of Christians you have known who were judgmental, hypocritical, and unloving. Some of the most insensitive, critical, judgmental, and mean-spirited people I've known were persons who claimed to be committed Christians.

I was officiating at the graveside funeral for a young man who had taken his own life. The parents were still in shock and experiencing intense grief. In the eulogy and message I sought to help them, and all who had gathered, to make sense of this terrible tragedy while finding in God comfort and hope. And we remembered the unique and special qualities of their son. Following the service a sister and brother-in-law of one of the boy's parents came to me and asked, "Why didn't you tell them that their son is in hell today?" I was taken aback and asked, "How do you know the boy is in hell today? Do you know what was in the boy's heart? Are you so certain you know the mind of God?" They looked at me and walked away. What kind of people are so certain of another's eternal fate that they can stand before grieving parents and callously tell them their son is in hell?

I could fill this book with story after story like this from my own personal experience of Christians, including a few pastors I know, who are free with their condemnation of everyone who doesn't conform to their very narrow view of the world, of the Bible, and of truth.

## JESUS AND THE PHARISEES

Of course, Jesus confronted the same kinds of things in his day. If you read the Gospels carefully, Jesus never got angry with prostitutes, adulterers, or ordinary "sinners." Nor did his actions turn such people away. In fact,

Jesus drew "sinners" to himself by the thousands. He made such people feel at ease. The only people Jesus had words of judgment for in the Gospels were the *religious* folks. What angered him the most about these people, particularly the religious leaders, was their judgmentalism, their hypocrisy, and their failure to love. They believed God was primarily interested in people following the rules. Jesus taught that God's primary rule was love, and that God's interest wasn't in condemning "sinners" but in drawing them to God.

Though Jesus was opposed by various people in the Gospels, his primary opposition was from the Pharisees, who believed that holiness and a life pleasing to God were found in separating themselves from sin and in obeying the commands of God. Although this makes sense, the Pharisees, like many modern-day Christians, had missed the point. They failed to see that God's primary concern is not rules, but people. They should have been celebrating the fact that thousands of people who had turned away from organized religion were drawn to hear Jesus teach about the kingdom of God. Instead they were *repulsed* by Jesus' willingness to associate with "sinners" (see Luke 15:2). In response, Jesus spoke some pretty harsh words to the Pharisees and the other religious leaders of his time. The word he used most frequently to describe them was the Greek word *hupokrisis* from which we get our word *hypocrisy*. This Greek word was used to refer to an actor in a play—a pretender.

The truth is, we're all in danger of being "pretenders" when it comes to our highest values and aspirations. This is particularly true for religious people, which is why Jesus warned his disciples on multiple occasions about hypocrisy, warnings that covered four different expressions of hypocrisy: wrong motives, judging others, "majoring in the minors," and being two-faced. Let's briefly consider what Jesus warned against in each of these areas.

### 1. Wrong Motives

Once when Jesus was talking to his followers, he warned them about the dangers of praying, fasting, and helping the poor for the wrong reasons. He talked about people who would pray on street corners, blow a loud trumpet when they were about to give to a needy person, and make sure everyone who saw them knew they were fasting so that others would know how "religious" they were and praise them for it. Their desire was not to grow close to God or to humble themselves before God, but to gain attention and accolades and the praise of people. They were using God and their religion to further their careers or their stature in the community, or to meet their needs for affirmation from others.

> ## What Did Jesus Say?
>
> *"So whenever you give [help to the needy], do not sound a trumpet before you, as the hypocrites do in the synagogues and in the streets, so that they may be praised by others. Truly I tell you, they have received their reward. . . . And whenever you pray, do not be like the hypocrites; for they love to stand and pray in the synagogues and at the street corners, so that they may be seen by others. Truly I tell you, they have received their reward. . . . And whenever you fast, do not look dismal, like the hypocrites, for they disfigure their faces so as to show others that they are fasting. Truly I tell you, they have received their reward."*
>
> (Matthew 6:2, 5, 16)

Do we have a similar struggle today? Do we ever want someone to know that we are a Christian or that we go to a particular church because we think it will be good for our reputation, social standing, or career? Are we ever tempted to make sure people have noticed our good deeds or acts of piety? Do we ever desire to be in the spotlight—to be affirmed or praised or recognized? Of course we do! Most of us are a mixed bag of motives.

We need to continually ask ourselves this question: Am I using God, or am I allowing God to use me?

### 2. Pointing Out the Sin of Others Without Seeing Our Own

One day Jesus asked some religious leaders how they could criticize people who had a speck of sawdust in their eye when they didn't notice the two-by-four poking out of their own eyes (Matthew 7:1-5). He was referring to religious people who readily point out the sins of others while failing to see their own shortcomings. They demonstrate a kind of superiority and spiritual or moral pride, but they fail to see that their pride is actually a more sinister and deadly sin than the sins of those they are denouncing.

Jesus then called his hearers to remove the "log" from their own eye before seeking to remove the speck from another's eye. In

> ### What Did Jesus Say?
>
> *"Why do you see the speck in your neighbor's eye, but do not notice the log in your own eye? Or how can you say to your neighbor, 'Let me take the speck out of your eye,' while the log is in your own eye? You hypocrite, first take the log out of your own eye, and then you will see clearly to take the speck out of your neighbor's eye."*
>
> (Matthew 7:3-5)

essence, he was saying, "Stop pointing out the sins of others—you've got enough issues of your own!"

We might ask ourselves if we are ever guilty of the very thing Jesus denounced in the Pharisees. Often it happens after we become a Christian or make a new commitment to follow Christ. Suddenly we no longer want to do certain things. Perhaps we used to curse a lot, so we decide we will no longer do that. Pretty soon we have stopped cursing, and that's a good thing. Or maybe we say we will no longer drink, and eventually we get to the point where we are not drinking anymore. Again, that's a good thing.

However, as we free ourselves from certain destructive behaviors, often we begin to notice that others are still doing them. Before long we begin to feel good about ourselves because we no longer do those things. Then one day we find ourselves saying to someone, "Hey, have you noticed how much Sharon curses?" or "Can you believe how much Bill drinks?" Pretty soon we have traded cursing or drinking for being prideful, which is even more dangerous to the soul.

We need to ask ourselves this question: Do I point out other people's sins without recognizing my own?

### 3. Majoring in Minors

The Pharisees developed a complex and intricate set of laws to govern their daily life. The word *Pharisee* likely comes from a Hebrew word that means "separated" or "set apart." They wanted to be holy and righteous before God, which was a good motivation. But in determining what was required to please God, they created an oral law that ensured that righteousness was defined to the smallest detail. For example, when it came to the practice of tithing—giving a tenth of their income to God—they actually separated out a tenth of the clippings from their herb plants and contributed even that. No one was going to accuse them of not living up to their obligations!

But Jesus did. Just a few days before he was crucified, Jesus sternly rebuked the Pharisees. He reminded the Pharisees that it was well and good to tithe, even down to such a detailed level, *except* when, at the same time you forgot about important things like justice and mercy toward your neighbor and faith in God (Matthew 23:23-24). In their quest for theological orthodoxy and religious purity, the Pharisees forgot how to love.

Unfortunately, this kind of hypocrisy is still prevalent today. We Christians fight over forms of baptism, how we interpret Scripture, and the words we use in the Lord's Prayer. We cannot even fellowship with one another but choose to divide into different denominations. In times past, we fought entire wars over our sectarian differences.

## What Did Jesus Say?

*"Woe to you, scribes and Pharisees, hypocrites! For you tithe [the herbs in your herb garden but] have neglected the weightier matters of the law: justice and mercy and faith. . . . You blind guides! You strain out a gnat but swallow a camel!"*

(Matthew 23:23-24)

We need to ask ourselves this question: Have I forgotten Jesus' assurance that our love for one another is how the world will know we are his followers?

### 4. Being Two-faced

You probably know people who appeared to be one thing when you first met them, but upon getting to know them better you found they were something else entirely. Jesus knew them, too. Once he suggested that such people are like a person who washes the outside of a dirty cup but fails to wash the inside, so what drink remains inside the cup spoils (Matthew 23:25). I picture the glasses of milk and soda I used to find in my teenage daughter's room that had been sitting there for weeks—curdled, moldy, and the rankest of smells!

Jesus was speaking of a superficial faith, which is seen in the outward appearances of religious behavior but has not sunk down into the heart. Like those who focus on the minutiae, people like this have missed the bigger point of faith. Their religion is skin deep and hasn't addressed the really serious issues in their hearts—or the really important issues in society.

This description applies to too many Christians I know. They understand how to do religious things but fail to let their religion change their values, their hearts, and ultimately their daily lives. Their religion is window dressing.

## What Did Jesus Say?

*"Woe to you, scribes and Pharisees, hypocrites! For you clean the outside of the cup and of the plate, but inside they are full of greed and self-indulgence. You blind Pharisee! First clean the inside of the cup, so that the outside also may become clean."*

(Matthew 23:25-26)

We see this theme throughout the Bible. Note God's frustration with the religious people of Isaiah's day:

> When you come to appear before me,
>     who has asked this from your hand?
>     Trample my courts no more; . . .

I cannot endure solemn assemblies with
    iniquity. . . .
they have become a burden to me,
    I am weary of bearing them.
When you stretch out your hands [in prayer],
    I will hide my eyes from you;
even though you make many prayers,
    I will not listen;
    your hands are full of blood.
Wash yourselves; make yourselves clean;
    remove the evil of your doings
    from before my eyes;
cease to do evil,
    learn to do good;
seek justice,
    rescue the oppressed,
defend the orphan,
    plead for the widow. (Isaiah 1:12-17)

Remember that God was speaking to people who showed up for worship every weekend, said their prayers, and gave their tithes but somehow missed the point. God was expressing hatred for the people's worship services because they did all of this religious activity but did not have a heart for justice, failed to deliver mercy or compassion, and did not stand up for those who could not stand up for themselves. Could God make a similar statement about the church today?

I think many of us have a tendency to focus on the superficialities. We allow our faith to go only skin deep; it never penetrates our hearts or our values. It's easy to be a Christian for an hour or two one day a week. It's not even that hard to pretend to live the Christian life on a superficial level. The challenge comes in living out what we say we believe—in caring about the things that matter to God and changing our values and our lifestyles so that God's work is accomplished in our world.

We need to ask ourselves this question: Have I cleaned the outside of the cup but neglected the inside?

## WE ARE ALL RECOVERING PHARISEES

If Pharisees are religious people who struggle with wrong motives, with being critical and judgmental of others, with missing the point, and with being two-faced, then I have a confession to make: I am a recovering Pharisee who often falls off the wagon. Everyone I know, religious people and atheists alike, struggle with these four tendencies.

It is so easy to do the right things for all the wrong reasons. It is so easy to point out the sins of others while ignoring our own. Most of us are experts at "majoring in the minors" while failing to do the really important things God demands of us. And which of us has never put on a face and pretended to be something we're not? It's only in recognizing our tendency to be Pharisees that we have any hope of remaining in recovery.

My experience with non-religious people is that they are not expecting Christians to be perfect. In fact, one young adult said, "I don't mind that you Christians don't live up to your ideals. I don't live up to all of my ideals either. In the end, I guess we're all hypocrites, it's just that I and my friends recognize that we're hypocrites. It seems that many Christians haven't figured this out yet." What makes the hypocrisy of Christians the more onerous is when we go about pointing out the sins of others.

## GETTING IT RIGHT

Every Christian gets it wrong sometimes. Still, the critique of non-Christians that they perceive us to be judgmental, hypocritical, and unloving should serve as a wake-up call to all of us—a warning to Christians who are becoming the very Pharisees Jesus preached against.

When we Christians act in ways that are judgmental, hypocritical, insensitive, and mean-spirited, we are acting in ways that are *un*christian. When describing what Christians should strive for, the apostle Paul used these words: love, joy, peace, patience, kindness, generosity, faithfulness, gentleness, and self-control (Galatians 5:22-23). Unchristian Christians stand out because even non-Christians know that these people are living in a way that is inconsistent with Jesus' teaching. Jesus commanded his followers not to judge. He warned them against hypocrisy. Again and again he called them to love all—both their neighbors and those with whom they did not see eye to eye.

For all the Christians who get it wrong, I believe there are many who get it right. They are not as vocal as their pharisaic counterparts. And they are not perfect. But there really are countless Christians who daily seek to live authentic lives of faith. They go out of their way to care for others. They are compassionate. They live and give sacrificially towards others. They volunteer their time to serve the poor, or visit the sick, or take the time to encourage the discouraged. They work for justice. They genuinely love people.

I think of Paul, a former Fortune 500 CFO, who gives hundreds of hours each year with our church to work rehabbing inner city schools to create bright and cheerful places for the poorest children in Kansas City to learn. I think of Kathy, the woman who cuts my hair. She volunteers each month to cut the hair of the homeless—people that she has befriended and come to love. She tells me she hopes and prays that her hands, and her haircuts, are a way of showing love to them and helping them believe their lives have value and meaning. I could go on for pages with stories like these of people who are a living testimony of what Christianity looks like when Christians get it right.

When I asked my friends on Facebook if they had other examples of Christians who get it right, I received dozens of remarkable stories. One was from a man named Chuck who wrote,

> Adam, my wife died about 10 years ago in a car accident in Tennessee. As I was being treated at a local hospital, the chaplain called a couple of local churches, letting them know there was a family from Kansas that had been in an accident. Mom was dead, dad was injured, and there were two small children, both under three. Shortly, one church sent several lay people to be with us and play with my sons while the pastor's wife rounded up some new clothes for me (mine were ruined), as well as overnight clothes for me and clothes and diapers for the boys since the salvage yard where the vehicle had been towed to was closed for the night. Another local church pastor showed up to offer us comfort. These people sacrificed a Friday night to come offer nothing but compassion, comfort, and support for some family from Kansas that they didn't know. . . . I will never forget the kindness of the people of Jasper, TN, and South Pittsburg, TN, as long as I live.

When we Christians get it right, we love and give, work for justice, and demonstrate kindness. When we Christians get it right, we, like Jesus, befriend those who are outside the church rather than condemning them. And when we Christians get it right, people are drawn to, rather than repelled by, our faith.

# 2

# CHRISTIANS, SCIENCE, AND POLITICS

*In the beginning when God created the heavens and the earth, the earth was a formless void and darkness covered the face of the deep, while a wind from God swept over the face of the waters. Then God said, "Let there be light"; and there was light. And God saw that the light was good; and God separated the light from the darkness. God called the light Day, and the darkness he called Night. And there was evening and there was morning, the first day. And God said, "Let there be a dome in the midst of the waters, and let it separate the waters from the waters." So God made the dome and sepa-rated the waters that were under the dome from the waters that were above the dome. And it was so. God called the dome Sky. And there was evening and there was morning, the second day.*

*(Genesis 1:1-8)*

*"Teacher, we know that you are sincere, and teach the way of God in accordance with truth, and show*

> *deference to no one; for you do not regard people*
> *with partiality. Tell us, then, what you think. Is it*
> *lawful to pay taxes to the emperor, or not?"* . . . *He*
> *said to them, "Give . . . to the emperor the things*
> *that are the emperor's, and to God the things that*
> *are God's." When they heard this, they were*
> *amazed; and they left him and went away.*
>
> (Matthew 22:16-17, 21-22)

Two areas where many young adults feel Christians get it wrong are science and politics—and sometimes these two areas intersect, as our views on one subject impact the other. We will explore each topic separately in this chapter, beginning with science.

Several years ago I sat down with a twenty-four-year-old soldier named John who had just returned from the war in Iraq. John was an Army Airborne Ranger who had been part of the initial invading forces in Afghanistan in 2001 and then in Iraq in 2003. His father told me that John had rejected Christianity and was passionate about his antipathy towards the Christian faith. He asked if I would talk with John. We had been talking for over an hour, when he said,

> The whole question of creationism versus evolution and scientific theory is always something that bothered me. You know the fact that people will tell you God created all of this ten thousand years ago in the blink of an eye; there you go. But when you honestly look at science and evolution—the miraculous complexity of it all and the beauty of how the system works—I've actually asked people, "Don't you see anything divine in that?" "Oh no, no, no." And people will pass off the creation story in the blink of an

eye, because its accepted and it's in the Bible. Well you know what, there are a lot of things that are in the Bible that were written two thousand years ago; and how can we honestly interpret what those men were saying in modern terminology? When people tell me creationism is in the Bible, that is just a statement to me of how exceedingly ignorant someone is. I don't like to blatantly label people as idiots, but I think of them as less intellectually active.

This is the perception many thinking people today have of Christians, that they are "less intellectually active." To understand how they have come to this perception of us, let us travel back to a day in history that many believe was the beginning of the modern divide between faith and science.

## SCIENCE, FAITH, AND FEAR

On June 22, 1633, a tribunal of the Roman Catholic Church pronounced Galileo a heretic for promoting a scientific idea that contradicted the church's teaching. Galileo loved God, and he loved science. He created a very primitive telescope and began studying the stars and the movement of the planets. His studies led him to the conclusion that Copernicus was right: the earth rotated around the sun. At the time, the church taught that the sun rotated around the earth, which they believed was stationary. They taught this because the Bible said that the "world is firmly established; it shall never be moved" (1 Chronicles 16:30; Psalm 93:1; 96:10). They concluded that the earth must be the center of the universe. Believing Galileo's teachings to be heresy, the tribunal made this pronouncement:

Galileo . . . you . . . have rendered yourself in the judgment of this Holy Office vehemently suspected of heresy, namely, of having believed and held the doctrine—which is false and contrary to the sacred and divine Scriptures—that the Sun is the center of the world and does not move from east to west and that the Earth moves and is not the center of the world; and that an opinion may be held and defended as probable after it has been declared and defined as contrary to the Holy Scripture.[2]

They made Galileo take back what he had said (which he he seems to have done with his fingers crossed behind his back), and then placed him under house arrest to prevent him from spreading any more dangerous ideas.

Today, of course, it's common and accepted knowledge that the sun sits at the center of our solar system, and that there are likely countless other solar systems with planets also circling their own stars spread among ours and all the other galaxies flung throughout the universe. In other words, what was a dangerous and heretical idea on June 22, 1633, is now something most people, including most Christians, take for granted.

Galileo's trial was the start of an accelerating process in which scientific discoveries have drawn the wrath of Christians who complain that the new ideas undermine their faith. From discoveries in geology about the age of the earth to the much-maligned science of evolution, some Christians have been pushing back at advances in science for centuries.

Surveys of young adults show that many bright, thinking people find themselves increasingly alienated by the belief of some Christians that much of what we know from modern science is incompatible with Christian teaching. David Kinnaman had this to say about the Barna Institute's findings:

We found in our interviews of young non-Christians . . . a great deal of criticism for the church about its perceived anti-intellectual stance, that, when it comes to science or creation, evolution, or intelligent design, that the church was somehow behind the times. There is a great deal of skepticism . . . on the full range of science meeting faith, and they don't see many examples of Christians who are in vocations of science. A lot of times we say, well, let's be sheltered and live in a bubble about everything, because we think something out there might threaten our faith.

I think Kinnaman is right in his assessment that fear plays a major role in shaping how some Christians approach science. They want to be sure their children do not come in contact with the latest scientific theories or ideas that differ from their own because they're afraid that their faith may not be able to withstand the questioning. Simply put, they are afraid that science will disprove or debunk what they believe. They secretly worry that the next scientific development will be the one that decisively shows that God does not exist or that the gospel is a fraud. They think that the more people know about science, the less they will believe in God. They fear science because they think that either it competes with faith or is actively engaged in destroying faith. They think that science leaves no room for God, and that if you let it get its foot in the door, it will take over the whole house.

These fears motivate some Christians to take certain positions on biblical interpretation—on the relationship between science and faith—that are actually a losing proposition for the gospel. They wind up treating the Bible as a science textbook, insisting that any scientific theory that does not conform to it is in error. This leaves a lot of young adults, even those who've grown up in the church, a bit confused and feeling as though they have to choose between faith and science. A young adult named Emily described the dilemma this way:

> It's hard for a lot of Christians sometimes to really struggle with having to figure out how evolution really fits in with Bible and where did dinosaurs come in there. The excuse we've heard for so long is, "you've got to have faith." Unfortunately, when people want proof and they want science and religion to line up, and when it doesn't the excuse of "you've just got to have faith" is not exactly encouraging us to spend more time in the church and read our Bibles.

### Two Points of Debate: Creation and Evolution

One of the major points of debate has been the Genesis account of Creation. Some Christians have insisted that science must conform itself to a literal reading of the verses in Genesis. I find this odd. The Genesis account is not meant to teach us *how* God created but *that* God created. God did not say to the author of Genesis, "Let me give you a lecture on how I created the universe. Make sure you get this down perfectly and tell everyone else, because I want them to understand how it all happened." That was not the point.

Actually, when we read the Creation account in Genesis, we find that it lines up with the cosmological understandings of the ancients. They understood that the earth was square or rectangular and flat, and that it was laid upon foundations under which there was water. This was self-evident to them because they observed that when they dug a well, they found water. They believed the earth with its four corners was laid upon a sea of water—the abyss—and if you stepped off the edge of the earth, you stepped into the abyss. They also believed there was water over the earth in the skies. They pictured the atmosphere as a dome, and in the first realm of the dome were the stars, the sun, and the moon. Beyond that they believed there were more waters. All of this is captured in the story of Creation.

The ancients also had a different understanding of how things happened. So we read in the Genesis account that there was light and darkness on day 1. On day 2, God created the atmosphere for the earth. On day 3, God created vegetation. Then, on day 4, God finally created the sun. How did it happen that way? How does that fit together? Well, if we're focusing on these details, we have missed the point.

God was not concerned that the ancients believed that space was made up of water, or that the earth was flat, or that there was something like a dome covering the earth. God was not concerned that they believed the earth was formed and then vegetation and then the sun. God knew we would figure out the science. What had to be communicated was the theology—specifically, that there was a God who is the author

## What Did Jesus Say?

Two times in the Gospel of Mark, Jesus makes a reference to God's act of creation. In each instance, Jesus acknowledges the most important point of the Genesis account: *that* God created.

*"But from the beginning of creation, 'God made them male and female.'"*
(Mark 10:6)

*"For in those days there will be suffering, such as has not been from the beginning of the creation that God created until now, no, and never will be."*
(Mark 13:19)

of life, that creation is God's good gift, and that human beings were formed in God's image.

Science cannot teach us about the meaning of life or its goodness. It cannot teach us about the meaning of human existence or our purpose for being here. Scripture and faith teach us these lessons. Science, on the other hand, teaches us about how things unfold. It teaches us about how creation works. It gives us scenarios related to how the universe developed or how life evolved.

This brings us to a second point of debate: evolution. In the past century, Christians were often known for their opposition to evolution. Not all Christians were opposed to evolution, but it seemed that the most vocal Christians were. They felt that evolution (at least at the "macro" level) somehow undermined the glory of God. They believed that God had to have created each species, from scratch, rather than overseeing a process by which simpler life forms became more complex. The most famous of the battles between Christianity and evolution was played out in a courtroom in Dayton, Tennessee, in July 1925. In March of that year the Tennessee legislature had made it illegal to teach any theory that contradicted the creation of humankind as taught in the Bible. While Christian attorney William Jennings Bryan won the case, and high school teacher John Scopes was found guilty of breaking the law, the constitutionality of the law was upheld. It was not repealed until 1967. Bryan may have won the case, but it was Christianity that appeared the loser. In the latter part of the twentieth century, the battle was on again as fundamentalists challenged textbooks and demanded that creationism be taught alongside evolution.

Yet to many Christians, evolution is simply a way of describing a process that God established for creating the magnificent forms of life we have today. Henry Ford designed the automobile assembly line. He approved the designs of his cars. His name appears on every car. Yet he did not personally build each car. They were his design. His fingerprints were all over the process. Millions of Fords were produced during his watch over the company. No one said that because Ford didn't personally build each car with his own hands he wasn't ultimately responsible for the Ford automobile: no Henry Ford, no Ford Automobile Company. In the same way, God created the processes and the plans for progression of life on our planet. Whether each species was individually crafted by God or the result of a process God designed matters little to me. God remains the Creator either way.

Many Christians continue to be threatened by the idea of evolution, but God is not threatened by Darwin's theories. Again, evolution is only a description of a process that seems to explain how simpler organisms may evolve into more complex life forms over time. It is not incompatible with Christianity until the theory is misused and applied to ethics, or until someone uses it to suggest that there is no purpose or order to creation. I am one of millions of Christians who believe that the two are not incompatible.

### Science Helps to Magnify God

No, God is not threatened by evolution—or by any other scientific idea or discovery. And God does not want us to be threatened, either. If creation is the handiwork of God, then science helps us to see the exquisite and marvelous workings of creation. As people of faith, how can that do for us anything other than magnify God?

Several years ago I had the opportunity to visit the Sistine Chapel in Rome. As I stood there looking up at

Michelangelo's magnificent frescoes on the chapel ceiling, a docent come up and asked if I'd like to know more about the work. I said, "Please. I know a little, but I'd like to know more!" She told me that Michelangelo labored for four years to complete this work, and that it is considered one of the most important works in the history of art. She described techniques Michelangelo used, some of which he pioneered, in order to leave such a legacy. She even told me that one of the "facts" I had always been taught about the painting was wrong—Michelangelo did not lie on his back to paint; he stood on the scaffolding and cocked his head back (a far more uncomfortable position)! Do you think I was less in awe by virtue of having the docent's explanations? The docent's insights and knowledge led me to an immensely greater appreciation of the Sistine Ceiling and Michelangelo's artistry.

In the same way, scientists act as God's docents, whether they believe in God or not. By helping us understand God's handiwork, they add to the majesty and glory of creation that, as a believer, leaves me with a greater sense of awe about the One who created all things.

I am an amateur astronomer. Thanks to advances in our ability to magnify the night sky, I know something Galileo didn't understand: our sun is not actually the center of the universe but just a tiny little star in the Milky Way Galaxy with somewhere around four hundred billion other stars. And this galaxy is moving through space with hundreds of billions of other galaxies. On warm nights, I like to take my 8" Meade LX90 Schmidt-Cassegraine telescope out to my backyard to tour the galaxy. I begin with a glance at Saturn's rings and Jupiter's moons. Then I head off to the Hercules Cluster and then view a variety of nebula, stars, and galaxies. I turn my scope towards the Milky Way's nearest neighbor, the Andromeda Galaxy. Through my scope it is only a small gray smudge. But here's what I find mindboggling: The light in that smudge took two million years to reach my eye, travelling at the rate of 186,000 miles per second! And this is our nearest neighbor—part of the "local group" of galaxies.

As I stand in the darkness of my backyard and contemplate all of this, I feel small; and that leads me to realize how truly big God is. Astronomy leads me to say with the psalmist, "The heavens are telling the glory of God" (Psalm 19:1). I stand in the backyard and find myself driven to awe and wonder and praise.

## What Did Jesus Say?

" 'You shall love the Lord your God with all your heart, and with all your soul, and with all your mind.' This is the greatest and first commandment."

(Matthew 22:37-38)

Jesus said that we are to love and worship God with all that we are, including our minds. Isn't it exciting to realize that science can actually be a catalyst for worshiping God with all our minds by helping us to see how powerful and creative and awesome our Creator God truly is?

We get it wrong as Christians when we see science as a threat to our faith, or when we try to make the Bible a scientific textbook. But we get it right when we see science as an important companion in the quest for knowledge and truth and a catalyst for our worship of a magnificent God.

## POLITICS AND RELIGION

Another area where many young adults feel Christians get it wrong is politics. One young woman shared her story with me in an e-mail:

> I did not grow up in church; in fact I did not go to church at all until I was 25 years old. . . . I found myself supporting (primarily) Democrats running for office because I believed they supported issues I was deeply concerned about: poverty, education, the environment, health care. When I started attending church, it seemed to me that many of my social concerns would also have been concerns for Jesus. I was therefore surprised at the reaction my political beliefs drew [from some of the Christians I met]. . . . As a very new Christian, I thought I had perhaps done something wrong; I was given the impression that one could not be both a Democrat and a Christian.

This young woman who had recently joined the faith was told, in essence, that her kind wasn't welcome. *What kind of church would do such a thing? I wondered. Don't churches want people from outside the faith to join? Aren't committed and idealistic young folks like her precisely the sort of people churches should be reaching out to?* In response, I wrote back to ask what church she was attending. To my surprise, she said that she had joined the church I pastor!

I pastor a church in a predominantly Republican state, yet our congregation is divided between Democrats and Republicans. We have leaders and elected officials from both parties. I appreciate some elements of both parties and disagree with others. I have voted for persons in both parties. And I am convinced that Jesus would not perfectly fit either party.

Neither the Republican Party nor the Democratic Party has a corner on the truth, and it is a dangerous thing when the church becomes "married" to either political party. This danger is as present in churches on the left that marry the Democratic Party as it is in churches on the right who marry the Republican Party. When

Christianity becomes embedded within power politics, it is the church and the mission of Jesus Christ that lose.

What I believe has been so damaging in the area of politics for many young adults is the way that Christians sometimes engage in politics. I received this note from one of our older parishioners when I asked about how Christians get it wrong in politics:

> Your question caused a rush of memories of our most recent national political campaign. We have a number of very close friends who are passionate about their politics. They regularly profess their strong Christian commitments, but somehow have a blind spot when it comes to how they react to views and opinions of those with whom they differ. . . . When we get close to that political arena, I have trouble sensing any Christian love or tolerance of any perspective but their own.

Some Christians, in the name of God, say and do things in the realm of politics that are the antithesis of the gospel: slander, gossip, malicious talk, mean-spirited rhetoric, disrespect, and worse. This has been particularly true when it comes to spreading rumors and half-truths using the Internet. I've been disappointed at how often Christians I know forward slanderous e-mails to everyone on their e-mail list without taking the time to verify the claims in the message. It doesn't matter whether you are a Democrat or a Republican, you have a moral and spiritual responsibility not to slander or to send out inflammatory e-mails about the opposing party or its candidates.

The apostle Paul offers instructive words for how we Christians are meant to conduct ourselves in all areas of life. These words are particularly pertinent when it comes to politics:

Let no evil talk come out of your mouths, but only what is useful for building up, as there is need, so that your words may give grace to those who hear. And do not grieve the Holy Spirit of God, with which you were marked with a seal for the day of redemption. Put away from you all bitterness and wrath and anger and wrangling and slander, together with all malice, and be kind to one another, tenderhearted, forgiving one another, as God in Christ has forgiven you. (Ephesians 4:29-32)

Paul notes that when we act in unloving and unkind ways, we grieve the Holy Spirit of God. The Greek word for *grieve* means to "inflict distress or intense sadness upon." That is what we do to God when we speak words that tear others down, that slander others. We are called to speak words that "give grace"—undeserved kindness.

Jesus also gave us an important word about politics. It was the last week of his life, and the Pharisees and the teachers of the law were trying to find a way to trip him up. They decided to test him, and so they sent the Herodians to ask a question. The Herodians were Jews, but they were defined by their allegiance to King Herod and his successors. By the very name they went by, it was apparent that politics came before God. The question they asked Jesus was about paying taxes, and it was masterfully designed to put Jesus in a no-win situation. They asked, "Is it lawful for us to pay taxes to Caesar?"

The Jewish homeland was occupied by the Romans, who extracted great taxes from the Jewish people. The people hated the taxes, and they hated the occupation. They believed the Messiah would overthrow the Romans and the taxes would stop, and many of them thought that Jesus was the Messiah. The Herodians knew that the people resented paying taxes. If Jesus affirmed the payment of taxes, the people would turn away from him because they were looking for a Messiah who would overthrow the Romans. If he said no, the religious authorities would turn him over to the Roman governor as an enemy of the state for encouraging other people not to pay their taxes, and he would be put to death.

Jesus asked to see a coin. The coin had the image of Caesar on it. He asked, "Whose image is this?" They replied, "Caesar's." Jesus told them to give to Caesar the things that belong to Caesar and to God the things that belong to God. When he asked whose image was on the coin, the Greek word he used for image was *eikona*. It is the word used in the Greek translation of the Creation story where we read, "So God created humankind in his image, in the image of God he created them; male and female he created them" (Genesis 1:27).

Some think Jesus was simply being wise and tricky in telling them to give to Caesar the things that are Caesar's and to God the things that are God's, but I don't think it was merely a wise answer. I believe he was telling us something important. There are certain things in Caesar's, or the government's, realm—money, politics, and elections. We give those to the government—that is, we do our duty. But just as Caesar's image is on the coin, so God's image is on our souls. We were created in the image of God, and our souls belong to God. We must not confuse our allegiance to a political party or to the state with our faith in God. There

> ### What Did Jesus Say?
>
> *"Give therefore to the emperor the things that are the emperor's, and to God the things that are God's."*
> (Matthew 22:21)

is plenty in both parties that God would take issue with. We must not allow a party, or a leader, or even our nation to become for us an idol. Instead, we must give to God our allegiance—our souls and our hearts.

As followers of Jesus Christ, by necessity we belong to the one who made us, whose image we bear. So when we are involved in the civic arena, our hearts belong to God. For many Christians who are involved in politics, this does not seem to be the case. Their hearts really seem to belong to their nation or their political party, with God either in second or third place. But God says, "I won't share. You're going to be on this earth for a short period of time, but you will be in my kingdom forever." We are citizens of God's kingdom, yet for a time we also are citizens of this country. Our task is to seek to be a blessing and to live out our faith, always giving our primary allegiance to the One who made us.

I encourage all Christians to be engaged in the political arena. We should register, vote, run for office, and be involved in the important issues of our time. We are meant to work for a common good and to strive to see our communities, states, and nation look like God's heavenly kingdom. But we must be careful not to "get it wrong." When we get it wrong in the area of politics, we too closely associate our faith with a particular political party, or we lay aside Christian ethics and Christ's call to love even our enemies and instead engage in slander and mean-spirited partisan politics.

When we get it right, on the other hand, we work for justice with grace, truth, and love. We fight for what we believe in a way that is consistent with our faith. As Martin Luther King, Jr. once said, "Darkness cannot drive out darkness: only light can do that. Hate cannot drive out hate: only love can do that."[3] If we believe we are in the right about something, we pursue the right, but we do it with love rather than slander and disrespect. Finally, and most importantly, we give our total allegiance to God and God alone.

## A FINAL WORD ABOUT GETTING IT RIGHT IN SCIENCE AND POLITICS

One thing that can help us to get it right in both science and politics is to be open-minded. When we are closed-minded, refusing to listen to others' ideas or treating those who hold opposing viewpoints with contempt, we are not modeling a Christ-like attitude. But we show the patience, understanding, and love of Christ when we are teachable and show respect to others—when we act with kindness and are "quick to listen, slow to speak, slow to anger" (James 1:19). We are teachable when, with humility, we recognize that we do not have all the truth.

I've come to notice one thing as I've studied people who are mature—intellectually, emotionally, and spiritually. The more they grow in their faith and the more profoundly they know God, the more they know that they do not know! That is the kind of mindset we all need if we want to get it right in science and politics.

# 3

# WHEN SPEAKING OF OTHER RELIGIONS

*"Finally, all of you, be like-minded, be sympathetic, love one another, be compassionate and humble. Do not repay evil with evil or insult with insult. On the contrary, repay evil with blessing, because to this you were called so that you may inherit a blessing. . . . Always be prepared to give an answer to everyone who asks you to give the reason for the hope that you have. But do this with gentleness and respect."*

*(1 Peter 3:8-9, 15, TNIV)*

Charlie and Anthony are two of many young adults who feel that Christians sometimes get it wrong in the way they talk about other religions. This is what they had to say:

Sometimes there are certain Christians who [think] . . . if you are not a Christian, you are in the wrong. . . . Christians decide who to hate, and then they latch on to it. (Charlie)

I had an issue with some of them in high school. There was a Christian group . . . of kids who would non-stop talk about how terrible the Muslim faith was, how terrible Islam was . . . Jewish kids would be picked on. What got me was some of my really good friends eventually joined that group, and it felt like from that time on [they thought], "Oh, forget him; he doesn't believe in God. Anthony is going to go to hell." (Anthony)

Their comments can help us to hear three different issues, each stemming from how Christians talk about and act toward those who are not Christians.

First is the issue of how Christians often make others feel excluded. Anthony said that after some of his friends became Christians, they no longer wanted to be his friends. Another young person once asked me, "When did Christians become snobs? How did that happen?" Unfortunately, that is precisely the perception some people have when they feel rejected and excluded by Christians.

Second is the issue of how many Christians speak about and act toward people who practice other world religions. Though most of us would never use the word *hate* to describe our feelings toward people of other religions, the way we talk about other religions often leads young people to think that, unlike Jesus, we are both unkind and uncharitable.

Third is the ease with which some Christians make statements about who's going to hell. I've had several people tell me I should go to hell, but I've only had one person ever tell me that I was going to hell—and it was not a pleasant experience. It certainly did not make me very receptive to hear what else the individual had to say.

In this chapter we will address all three of these issues by considering two questions: "How wide is God's mercy?" and "What kind of witness will you be?"

## HOW WIDE IS GOD'S MERCY?

Some Christians say that everyone who does not believe just as they do is on the fast track to hell—and they usually have plenty of Scripture to back them up. If your personal relationship with Jesus Christ does not look like theirs does, or if you weren't baptized in the same way that they were, or if you don't hold to the same interpretations of Scripture that they do, then they do not believe you are part of the true church.

One night I was preparing to head out the door when the doorbell rang. I opened the door, and there stood a man in his late sixties, holding a Bible in one hand and a small child in the other. He told me that he was going door to door to remind people that Jesus was a man with important things to say. I asked if he would like to come in, and he and his one-year-old granddaughter stepped inside. He told me that the Bible talks about Jesus, and that he believes it is important to read the Bible. I said, "That's terrific. I think so, too." I introduced myself to him and told him I was a pastor, and then I asked about his church. He said that he was a Jehovah's Witness. Realizing that I am a pastor, he shifted gears and wanted to talk about one of the key doctrines on which traditional Christianity and the Jehovah's Witnesses differ: the Trinitarian conception of God. They do not believe that God is Father, Son, and Holy Spirit. They believe that Jesus was the first being created by God, but that he is not divine. After trading Scriptures back and forth for a bit, I finally said, "I suspect that it is unlikely that I'm going to persuade you to leave your church, and seeing that I have spent years studying this issue, it is unlikely that you will persuade me to become a Jehovah's Witness. But I want to ask you something: Do you love God?"

He said, "I do," and I said, "I do, too."

Then I asked, "Do you trust Jesus as your Savior and seek to follow him as your Lord?"

He replied, "I do."

Again I said, "I do, too."

Then I said, "I'm persuaded that my brain is too small to fully comprehend the mystery of God. But I'm willing to say that because you love God and you strive to follow Jesus Christ as your Lord that we're going to see each other in heaven. And when we get there, I have a feeling we will find that neither of us was completely right in our understanding of the nature of God. But there's something I want you to know: Even though we differ on a significant theological point—something we both think is very important—I admire your courage, your commitment to the gospel as you understand it, and your desire to study Scripture and to follow Jesus."

I don't think he was sure what to make of that. My hope was, first, to bless him and, second, to invite him to consider that perhaps God is bigger than either of us supposes.

You may be unsettled that I said he would actually be in heaven. After all, Jehovah's Witnesses do not hold to a Christine doctrine that is very, very important. I am not saying that doctrine does not matter. In fact, doctrine matters a great deal. However, when Jesus called people to be his disciples, he did not say, "First take systematic theology I and II, and then come and follow me." He simply said, "Follow me, and I will make you fish for people" (Matthew 4:19). So as I see it, God's mercy is wide enough for him, even though I disagree with his theological assumptions. And that goes for a bunch of other folks, too.

What do you think? How wide is God's mercy? Will God consign to hell those who call upon the name of Jesus as Savior and Lord but who do not get their theology exactly right? Is having a complete and correct theology essential to our salvation? Or does God look at the heart and see that our intent and desire is to love, follow, and serve God?

You might say, "Perhaps God's mercy is wide enough for people who call themselves Christians, but what about people of other religions?" How are we Christians to understand God's perspective on people of other religions—Jews, Muslims, Hindus, and others?

I am reminded of the comments of John, a young man I interviewed, who told me that one of the things that turned him off to Christianity was the way that many Christians talk about people of other faiths. This is what he told me:

> One of the things I have always had trouble swallowing with the Christian faith is that we have a God of compassion, a God of love, a God of forgiveness; but if you don't say, "Jesus, you're my savior," you're going to burn. Flat out. . . . That's not forgiveness, that's not compassion, that's coercion, that's blackmail. . . . People all over the world . . . could live the best life. They could be compassionate, they could be understanding, they could do their best to help their community, to help other people, to serve their nation . . . but you're going to tell me that this person who lived an idyllic life of straight moral value is going to go to hell just because he didn't say, "I love Jesus"? There's something there that is not right. There is something about that puzzle piece that doesn't fit in with what the Christian faith is trying to sell.

John and a whole generation of young adults have heard from many Christians that only those who have personally received Jesus Christ as Lord and Savior will enter heaven. That leaves at least 4.2 billion people who are going to hell. The folks who most loudly champion this view often do not believe that Catholics, Orthodox, or Mainline Protestant Christians are going to heaven, either. In that case, perhaps only 600 million people of the world's current population are going to heaven.[4] The rest will be tormented for eternity in hell because they either did not call upon the name of Christ or did not do so in the way that others felt was right. For John and many other young adults, this is a strange picture of a God who is said to love human beings deeply. The fate of non-Christians raises more questions than I will address here, including questions about hell, but primarily it raises questions about God's love, justice, mercy, and kindness.

I think young adults are right to question the wideness of God's mercy. I myself have questioned it, as have Christians in every age. For the purposes of our discussion, let me frame the question this way:

> *What is the eternal fate of those who earnestly seek God—who love God and seek to do what is right as best they understand it—but who either have not heard about Jesus or have not understood the gospel?*

Let us consider three ways that Christians through the ages have answered this question.

### 1. Christian Universalism

The first view is called Christian Universalism. (Note: This view is not the same as Unitarian Universalism.) Those who hold this view believe that all humankind ultimately will be reconciled to God, and that none will forever suffer in hell. Hell is seen as a temporary place with the primary focus of redemption rather than punishment. Hell's purpose is to lead people to repentance. Supporters of Christian Universalism claim that many of the most important theologians of the early church held this view.[5]

The idea of Christian Universalism solves several theological problems, including the idea of eternal torment, and that is appealing. The challenge it presents is that it removes human freedom to reject God's invitation of salvation. In other words, ultimately everyone will be forced to receive salvation and to dwell in heaven. Most Scriptures on the subject, however, point to the fact that God invites but does not force. God gives us choices.

## 2. Christian Exclusivism

A second view is Christian Exclusivism, or simply the Exclusivist view. Most of us are familiar with this view, which was championed by St. Augustine in the fifth century and by John Calvin in the sixteenth century. Today this view, or some variation of it, is held by most conservative Christians, a large number of moderate to conservative evangelicals, and some mainline Protestants.

According to this view, sin separates us from God, and only faith in Jesus Christ and his death upon the cross can set us right with God. Hence, without accepting Christ, one is still in a state of sin. A holy and righteous God cannot allow those living in sin to enter the heavenly kingdom. Therefore, anyone who has not personally trusted in Christ cannot enter heaven. Thus, by default, they are consigned to the place of the damned.

In its harshest, yet most consistent form, this view excludes from heaven all children who died without receiving Christ, those with mental disabilities who did not receive Christ, and any who have never heard the good news of Jesus Christ. I once asked a man who held this extreme view, "Are you suggesting that the Native Americans who lived on this continent for thousands of years before the first missionaries arrived were all sent to hell

## What Did Jesus Say?

*"For God so loved the world that he gave his only Son, so that everyone who believes in him may not perish but may have eternal life. Indeed, God did not send the Son into the world to condemn the world, but in order that the world might be saved through him. Those who believe in him are not condemned; but those who do not believe are condemned already, because they have not believed in the name of the only Son of God."* (John 3:16-18)

*"My sheep hear my voice. I know them, and they follow me. I give them eternal life, and they will never perish. No one will snatch them out of my hand."* (John 10:27-28)

*Jesus said to her, "I am the resurrection and the life. Those who believe in me, even though they die, will live, and everyone who lives and believes in me will never die."* (John 11:25-26)

*Jesus said to him, "I am the way, and the truth, and the life. No one comes to the Father except through me."* (John 14:6)

*"Everyone therefore who acknowledges me before others, I also will acknowledge before my Father in heaven; but whoever denies me before others, I also will deny before my Father in heaven."* (Matthew 10:32-33)

Other Scriptures commonly cited in support of Exclusivism:
Acts 4:11-12
Romans 1:16
Romans 3:20-26
Romans 10:9
1 John 2:23
1 John 5:11-12

even though they never had the opportunity to hear of Jesus Christ? We know many of them were deeply religious and sought God. Regardless of how they lived, how much they sought God, all of them—every man, woman, and child—was destined for hell without any opportunity to even call upon the name of Jesus Christ?" He responded that this was correct, that God could have revealed his Son to them in some other way, but barring that, they were in hell.

Like my young friend John, most young adults believe that something is not right with such an extreme view. It paints a picture of a God who is neither loving, just, or merciful. For this reason, many Christians today hold a more moderate Exclusivist view, believing that God will judge those who had absolutely no opportunity to receive Christ, including children and the mentally handicapped, according to how they responded to what they could know of God—to the light they were given.

I like that idea. Although it is not necessarily consistent with the first part of the argument, I resonate with that concept of God's mercy.

### 3. Christian Inclusivism

The exception held by moderate Exclusivists is expanded further in the third view: Christian Inclusivism. This view is the official position of the Roman Catholic Church and the generally accepted view of most mainline Protestants. Adherents to this view have included Justin Martyr, John Wesley, C. S. Lewis, John Stott, and in his later years, Billy Graham. It also is the view that makes most sense to me.

Like Exclusivists, Inclusivists believe that Jesus is the way, the truth, and the life. He is the source of salvation.

He died for the sins of the world. However, they believe that God can give this gift of salvation to anyone God chooses based upon the criteria God chooses. According to this view, it is possible for God to give the gift of salvation to those who have sought to love and serve God even if they have never heard the gospel or have not fully understood or accepted it. Inclusivists acknowledge that there are many people who have faith in God and a desire for salvation, but who may not fully understand where salvation comes from or the name by which salvation is given. They believe that in such cases, God looks at the heart and judges according to the light of the knowledge those persons have access to.

Inclusivism reminds us that the Christian gospel, the good news, is that we are saved by grace. In the New

## What Did Jesus Say?

*"Whoever is not against us is for us."* (Mark 9:40)

*"Indeed, God did not send the Son into the world to condemn the world, but in order that the world might be saved through him."* (John 3:17)

*"For the bread of God is that which comes down from heaven and gives life to the world."* (John 6:33)

*"And I, when I am lifted up from the earth, will draw all people to myself."* (John 12:32)

Other Scriptures commonly cited in support of Inclusivism:
Acts 10:34-35
Romans 2:6-16
Romans 5:18
Colossians 1:20
1 Timothy 4:10
2 Peter 3:9
1 John 2:2

Testament, grace refers to God's kindness, love, care, work on our behalf, blessings, gifts, goodness, and salvation. But it is more than that—it is *undeserved*. God's grace is pure gift.

The apostle Paul lays out the Christian conception of how salvation works in Ephesians 2:4-5, 8-9:

> God, who is rich in mercy, out of the great love with which he loved us even when we were dead through our trespasses, made us alive together with Christ. . . . For by grace you have been saved through faith, and this is not your own doing; it is the gift of God— not the result of works, so that no one may boast.

Salvation is by grace. It is not by what we know— though in tasting salvation we will want to know more. It is not by what we do—though the experience of salvation will lead us to act differently. We are saved by *God's* initiative because of *God's* love, *God's* righteousness, *God's* kindness, and *God's* mercy. All we bring to the table is faith. We trust that there is a God who loves us, who has called us, and who offers us the gift of salvation. Ideally this faith is in Jesus Christ, if we have had the opportunity to hear and understand the gospel. But many people have not had that opportunity.

So, the Inclusivist believes that for those who have not heard or understood the gospel message but who have sought God—to love God, to do what God desires—the very act of seeking God is an expression of faith. God looks at the heart and sees faith, and God responds with mercy and grace.

I would suggest that most Christians today—most Catholics and mainline Protestants and an increasing number of evangelicals—do not believe that all non-Christians will be sent to hell. This is my position as well.

I trust that God is kind, merciful, just, and loving. God knows the hearts of men and women, and God's judgment will be consistent with God's love.

Whenever I share this idea of Christian Inclusivism, someone inevitably asks, "Then why should we bother to share the gospel with people, if God may save them anyway? Why have so many missionaries risked their lives to offer Christ to people who did not know him?" I usually respond with several questions of my own: Do you mean to suggest that the only reason we share the good news of Jesus Christ is because we believe God will eternally torment people in hell if we don't tell them about Jesus? Is avoiding hell the only reason to become a Christian? Is Christianity really only about getting a ticket to heaven?

I tell others about Jesus Christ not because I'm afraid God will eternally torment them in hell if I don't persuade them to accept Christ; I share Jesus Christ with others because I believe that in him we see and understand who God is and who we are meant to be. I share Christ with others because I believe he teaches us about the love, mercy, and grace of God. From him we learn sacrificial love. In him we experience forgiveness and mercy. I tell others about Christ because I believe he is the way, the truth, and the life. I tell others about Christ because he has changed my life so that the richest and most meaningful parts of my life all are somehow made so by him. I share Christ with others because I want them to know that God already loves them, and that Christ offers us both the truth about God and God's will for humanity. I share Christ with others because in Christ we hear good news of God's message of sacrificial love, of forgiveness of sins, and of the hope of everlasting life.

## WHAT KIND OF WITNESS WILL YOU BE?

This brings us to the second question of the chapter: "What kind of witness will you be?" The majority of young adults today are turned off by the way that many Christians speak about their faith, cause others to feel excluded, demonstrate arrogance, refuse to listen to the thoughts and beliefs of others, and are dismissive of those who are not Christians. Clearly that form of witness turns people away from Christ.

I was struck by the comments of a young woman named Penny whose story Dan Kimball included in his book *They Like Jesus but Not the Church*. This is what she said:

> Why do Christians act so horribly self-righteous when they tell us they are the only true religion and everyone else who holds to other faiths is wrong? . . . Eastern religions were more attractive to me, because they focused more on being kind to others, loving other people of other spiritual beliefs even if they are different from you, treading lightly, and being humble. I think that was similar to the message of Jesus, ironically, but that's the opposite of what I experienced from church and Christians.[6]

Penny was right about kindness and love and humility being characteristic of Jesus.

In his first epistle, the apostle Peter was writing to Christians in churches throughout what is now Turkey. They were surrounded by a non-Christian culture. It was not only non-Christian; it actually was hostile to Christianity. The believers in these churches were being harassed for their unwillingness to worship the prevailing gods. The entire epistle was aimed at helping these Christians to witness to their faith in such a setting. Peter called them to be holy—that is, to do the right thing (1 Peter 1:16). He wrote, "Live such good lives among the pagans that . . . they see your good deeds and glorify God" (2:12, NIV). He told them to show "proper respect to everyone" (2:17, NIV), to love deeply, and to humble themselves, noting that "God opposes the proud but gives grace to the humble" (5:5, NIV). Read again these verses from 1 Peter:

> Finally, all of you, be like-minded, be sympathetic, love one another, be compassionate and humble. Do not repay evil with evil or insult with insult. On the contrary, repay evil with blessing. . . . Always be prepared to give an answer to everyone who asks you to give the reason for the hope that you have. But do this with gentleness and respect. (3:8-9, 15, TNIV)

The most powerful form of Christian witness is what we do when we express authentic love, compassion, mercy, and kindness toward others.

I am reminded of a church member whose neighbor acted in ways that were hurtful, yet she insisted on finding ways to bless her neighbor. When her neighbor's husband died, she not only brought meals but also cleaned the house. She continued to find small ways of caring for her neighbor two months later, when most of the woman's friends had stopped calling. She prayed for her neighbor and demonstrated true love for her. She modeled the words of St. Francis: "Preach the gospel always, and when necessary, use words." Her faith was so compelling that her neighbor eventually asked if she could go to church with her.

## What Did Jesus Say?

*"By this everyone will know that you are my disciples, if you have love for one another."*
(John 13:35)

54

My hope is that when non-Christians hear the word "Christians," they will not think of people who are arrogant, casually condemning others to hell and acting in ways that make others feel small and excluded. Instead, my hope is that when they think of us they will think of people who are thoughtful, caring, respectful, and kind— people who live their faith by showing compassion to others, serving the poor, giving sacrificially of themselves, and seeking to bless those around them. If we will do this, we will avoid being arrogant and, instead, will model humility, respect, and love. My prayer is that we Christians will be a people who preach the gospel always, and when necessary, use words with gentleness and respect.

# 4

# WHEN BAD THINGS HAPPEN

*Then Job replied:*
*"I have heard many things like these;*
*miserable comforters are you all!*
*Will your long-winded speeches never end?*
*What ails you that you keep on arguing?*
*I also could speak like you,*
*if you were in my place;*
*I could make fine speeches against you*
*and shake my head at you.*
*But my mouth would encourage you;*
*comfort from my lips would bring you relief."*

(Job 16:1-5, NIV)

Like all of us, young adults struggle to make sense of God when bad things happen. They also struggle with the kinds of remarks well-meaning Christians often make when others are suffering. Our theology about how God is at work in the world in the midst of suffering and what we say to comfort people who are hurting are integrally related, and we are wise to explore these two areas if we want to reflect Jesus through our example and witness.

## WHAT WE BELIEVE SHAPES WHAT WE SAY

Once, when speaking to my young and thoughtful friend, John, the young Army Airborne Ranger who had just returned from Iraq, he gave me eight reasons he was not a Christian. As he explained the first reason he has rejected God and the Christian faith, he said this:

> It was the last time I ever prayed. I sat on the edge of the aircraft carrier in the Arabian Sea and I looked out and said, "God, Allah, Buddha, I don't care if you don't like me. But if one of you is out there, look over my boys. That's all I ask." I got on the bird and left. And the first thing someone told me when I got back on the USS Kittyhawk was that my friend was dead. Over the years I remember thinking, *If there is a God who is loving and compassionate, why did he kill my friend?*

John's question—"Why did God kill my friend?"—is based on a theological assumption that many Christians hold: Everything that happens is God's will. It is not uncommon to hear people put it this way: "Everything happens for a reason." If that is true, then John's friend died because it was part of God's master plan; it happened according to the will of God. Even though he was killed by a bullet in the midst of warfare, ultimately it was God who determined that he would die. It's not a far leap from that statement, then, to say that God killed John's friend.

One day I went out for lunch, and I happened to be wearing a Church of the Resurrection sweatshirt. A young woman apparently noticed the shirt and recognized me to be a Christian. She approached me and said, "I have just one question. Why did God kill my sister?" Like John, her assumption was that God is in the business of choosing to take people's lives.

When we say that everything happens for a reason, we're saying that bad things—even tragic or evil things—happen because God intends for them to happen. The challenge that comes with this line of thinking is this: How can we trust, love, and desire to serve a God who wills or causes bad things to happen?

This question helps us to see at least part of the problem with an overly simplistic understanding of why bad things happen. An undeveloped or unexamined theology of evil and suffering can cause us to say things that are hurtful rather than helpful to those who are suffering. A woman in my congregation told me of her experience:

> Our baby died this past spring when he was six weeks old. So many Christians we have encountered since that time tell us "this was God's plan." . . . Before this tragic event, I guess I thought this was how life worked too. . . . But there is no way that the death of an innocent six-week-old and our inability to get pregnant again is part of some master plan. And if it is, then I'm simply not interested in the God that has that plan.

This woman did not believe that God willed the death of her child, yet well-meaning Christians continued to tell her that this was precisely what had happened—that the child's death was God's plan. Understandably, it became very difficult for her to conceive of following a God who would devise such a plan. She found herself struggling to reconcile the loss of her child and the goodness of God.

To be sure, it is no simple matter to reconcile a loving God with the suffering and pain in the world around us. Theologians speak of this as the "problem of evil" and call this area of inquiry *theodicy* (from the Greek *theo*, which means God, and *dike*, which means justice). People of faith have wrestled with this issue throughout the ages. Certainly, it is impossible for me to adequately unpack the topic in one chapter. My intent is not to provide *the* answer but to suggest a line of reasoning that may be helpful. To do this I will share a few central beliefs I have come to hold after more than thirty years of wrestling with the problem of suffering on a personal level, walking closely with many people who are suffering, and studying what the Scriptures and many theologians have to say on the subject. I would like to suggest that some of the long and commonly held assumptions about God's involvement in the affairs of our world—the things Christians sometimes say in the face of suffering and even blessing—not only may be wrong but also may serve to push people away from God.

So, I invite you to question the assumptions you may have been taught regarding God's relationship to both the evil and the good that happen in our world, to read and study what other others have to say on the subject, and to carefully consider what you believe. This process will have a significant impact not only on your theological understanding of why bad things happen, but also on how effective you will be in offering comfort to those who are hurting and in need. It is my hope that, ultimately, we may be Christians who get it right when it comes to how we speak and act in times of suffering.

## GOD'S INVOLVEMENT IN THE WORLD

God's involvement in the world and in our lives is called providence. What you believe about providence determines how you respond when bad things happen.

Do you believe God controls *everything* that happens? Does God control every cell within your body every second of every day? Does God control every atom in the universe? Does God control the stock market, making it go up or down on a given day based on God's will? Does God determine when and where every drop of rain will fall and every wind will blow? Does every storm develop on cue at the command of God? Does God direct every lightening bolt, draught, tornado, earthquake, hurricane, and tsunami? Does God control the direction and speed of every car on every road and every plane in the sky?

There are those who would answer yes to each of these questions, and often they do so by referring to God's "sovereignty." This is a term that means that God is the highest authority, there is no one to whom God reports and no one to whom God answers. God is the Supreme Ruler—the "King of the Universe." The universe is the rightful property of God, who created it. Nearly all Christians would agree that God is sovereign—the highest authority and not dependent upon anyone or anything else. In an attempt to glorify God, however, some people go too far. It is not enough for them to claim that God is the highest authority. They also claim that God is actually controlling every dimension of the creation. The logical end of this line of reasoning, as we will see, makes God a monster. I call this line of thinking the marionette view of divine providence.

### The Marionette View of Divine Providence

If God is controlling and manipulating all things, then God is like a puppet master. God is constantly pulling the strings, and we are merely puppets. Consider a simple example. Think of the last football game you watched. Did God will for one team to beat the other? Was the game predetermined? If so, it would not have mattered how good any of the players were or how hard anyone played during the game because God had fixed the game. Maybe God loved one team more than the other, or needed to punish the losing team or perhaps teach them a lesson. If that is true, what is the point of even playing the game?

I do not believe that God has predetermined everything that happens according to God's will and plan. In fact, the Bible seems to teach the opposite of this view. Most of what we read in the Bible is the story of human beings doing what God does not want us to do and God working to make things right. The very first story, which takes place in the garden of Eden, defines our relationship with God. In this story, God places the tree of the knowledge of good and evil in the midst of the garden and tells Adam and Eve not to eat from it. God does not want them to eat from the tree, but they choose to do so anyway. This story paints a picture of a God who gives us choices—free will—and allows us to play a role in determining what will happen in the future, even when our choices hurt God and are not what God wants to see happen.

Natural Disasters

To press the marionette view further, let us consider natural disasters. Some of the biblical authors wrote with the assumption that natural disasters are the handiwork of God. Nearly all ancients believed that to be true. With their limited scientific knowledge, it is not surprising that this was their conclusion when the ground shook or severe storms developed. But do we still believe today that every storm is an act of God? Some do.

Shortly after Hurricane Katrina struck the Gulf Coast, causing the death of more than 1,800 people and destroying the property, hopes, and dreams of tens of thousands of others, one Christian writer penned these words:

> Many thoughtful Americans are asking, "Why did this happen?" There is an answer to this question. . . . The answer is found in understanding that man is not in control. God is! Everything in the sky, the sea and on earth is subject to His control. Psalm 107:25-33 says, "He raiseth the stormy wind which lifted up the waves of the sea . . . He turns rivers into a desert, and springs of water into a thirsty ground; a fruitful land into a salt waste, because of the wickedness of those who dwell in it." Was there wickedness in New Orleans, Alabama and Mississippi? Well, let's see. There was the burgeoning Gulf Coast gambling industry, with a new casino that was to open on Labor Day weekend. . . . And then there was the 34th Annual gay, lesbian and transgender . . . Labor Day gala. . . . Further, there is the well-known corruption, drugs, and immoral playground of the French Quarter. . . ."[7]

His conclusion: Hurricane Katrina was an act of God intended to punish the people of the Gulf Coast because of the casinos, the gay pride parade, and the French Quarter. This assertion, however, raises several questions. Why was the French Quarter left standing? Why did thousands of the poor as well as good church-going people lose their homes? And why were the gambling casinos some of the first businesses to reopen?

Following the storm, news broadcasts on every channel depicted the devastating destruction. Was that destruction the handiwork of God? Is that the way God works? When we look to the testimony of the Scriptures, we see that God is just, loving, merciful, and kind. Would a just, loving, merciful, and kind God send a storm to indiscriminately wipe out entire neighborhoods—both the good and the bad—hundreds of miles from New Orleans because of a casino, a gay pride parade, and the French Quarter? It is true that the French Quarter is home to sinners and prostitutes, but Jesus—who was the perfect and complete representation of God—was a friend to sinners and prostitutes. He did not attack them but went into their homes and ate with them.

When I ask the "why" question about hurricanes, I look to the meteorologists. They know what causes them, and they can predict them. What's more, they tell us that hurricanes are a naturally occurring phenomenon critical to maintaining steady global temperatures. Earthquakes are another natural disaster essential to life on our planet. The ancients explained earthquakes by saying that the gods must be angry. Today we understand the flow of magma underneath the earth and the convection

## What Did Jesus Say?

*"There were some present who told him about the Galileans whose blood Pilate had mingled with their sacrifices. He asked them, 'Do you think that because these Galileans suffered in this way they were worse sinners than all other Galileans? No, I tell you; but unless you repent, you will all perish as they did. Or those eighteen who were killed when the tower of Siloam fell on them—do you think that they were worse offenders than all the others living in Jerusalem? No, I tell you; but unless you repent, you will all perish just as they did.' "*

(Luke 13:1-5)

Although Jesus was not discussing natural disasters, he was saying that those who were killed in these tragedies were not being punished by God because of their sin.

that moves tectonic plates, ultimately resulting in earthquakes. Given this knowledge and understanding, most people today would agree that natural disasters are acts of nature, not acts of God.

## Illness and Disease

Perhaps it seems logical to come to the conclusion that natural disasters are not the handiwork of God, but what about illnesses? How is God involved when sickness and disease touch our lives? This takes the question of divine providence to an even more personal level.

In his classic work *The Will of God*, British pastor Leslie Weatherhead wrote about talking with an Indian friend who had lost his son in a cholera epidemic. Weatherhead tried to comfort and console his friend, but the man responded, "Well, padre, it is the will of God. That's all there is to it." Knowing his friend well enough to reply without being misunderstood, Weatherhead asked, "Supposing someone crept up the steps onto the veranda tonight, while you all slept, and deliberately put a wad of cotton soaked in cholera germ culture over your little girl's mouth as she lay in that cot there on the veranda, what would you think about that?"

The friend answered that if someone attempted such a despicable thing and he caught the person, he would kill the intruder with as little compunction as he would a snake. Then he asked, "What do you mean by suggesting such a thing?"

Weatherhead replied, "Isn't that just what you have accused God of doing when you said it was his will?"

Weatherhead follows the story with this statement: "Surely we cannot identify as the will of God something for which a man would be locked up in jail, or be put in a criminal lunatic asylum."[8]

Once again we must turn to the Scriptures. Whatever we say about God or attribute to God must line up with God's character as revealed in the Scriptures. The character of God revealed throughout the Scriptures is that of a kind, loving, and merciful Father—not a monster. God does not inject cancer cells into people or cause other diseases—or take babies away from their mothers, or send cars careening into one another. Much of what we blame God for is the result of humanity's sin and the realities of an imperfect world—realities such as sickness, disease, natural disasters, accidents, violence, and death. God accepts these realities, but God does not initiate them.

## Some Difficult Questions

This brings us to some difficult questions. At this point in the discussion, some might interject,

*But don't bad things sometimes happen because God is trying to teach us something?*

The idea behind this question is that suffering is part of God's plan because God needs to discipline or teach us. I will answer this question by posing another question: Would you ever discipline your own children by disfiguring them, inflicting terrible suffering upon them, or killing them? If you did, you would be arrested, convicted, and thrown in jail. Jesus described God as a parent who was actually better than we are, not worse. Therefore, I do not believe that God causes tragedy in order to teach us a lesson. I do believe, however, that God uses the difficult and tragic experiences of our lives to grow us and make us more like Christ. There is a distinction between these two statements, and it is significant. I will say more about this at the end of this section.

"Okay," you might say, "perhaps God does not *cause* bad things to happen . . ." But there is an unanswered question that troubles you:

*If God is a good and loving parent, why doesn't God stop bad things from happening?*

A similar question is close behind it:

*Why, when bad things do happen, does God sometimes not answer our prayers for healing (or some other kind of deliverance)?*

These are the more difficult questions, in my opinion.

The deists believed that a good, loving, and just God had created a closed system. God created the world, set in motion the laws that govern it, and stepped away. You might say that God wrote the software code, closed the system, and determined never to interfere with the established laws so that order and predictability might be maintained. They believed that God watches and cares but does not intervene. The idea is that if God were to intervene here and there, suddenly the whole system could be thrown into chaos.

If you have ever watched the original *Star Trek* television show, you are familiar with what they called the prime directive. The Star Fleet officers would beam onto a planet, but their directive was never to interfere with what was happening on the planet because it would cause problems. I find this intellectually satisfying to a point, which is why I believe the deists were headed in the right direction. However, I believe they got off course when they said that God could never intervene, because that leaves no possibility for God to answer prayer in any palpable, tangible way. In fact, if taken to the extreme, that would mean that God could not even touch our hearts or speak to us in any way.

So, although deism may seem to be an easy answer to the question, it does not hold up to the testimony of the Scriptures or my own life experience. In the Scriptures, we see a God who is not distant but involved in the world and in the lives of God's children. My own personal experience validates that God is involved in the ways of our world and in my life. God speaks to me and touches my heart on a regular basis. There have been times when coincidences have been too coincidental. And on rare occasions, God has seemed to step in and suspend the very laws God established for purposes that neither I nor others could understand at the time.

I pray over thousands of prayer concerns each year, and in the past eighteen years I've only seen about half a dozen miraculous answers to prayer for which the doctors had no explanation. This track record is not unique to me. My observation is that God typically does not answer our prayers by intervening supernaturally. That is not God's usual way. Even so, God can intervene, and sometimes God does.

When God does choose to intervene, we do not always know why. It is not that God loves one person more than another. Perhaps some part of God's plan is dependent upon an individual being healed or touched in a miraculous way. Oftentimes we simply do not know why God does or does not choose to intervene.

I have had such an experience in my own life. When I was sixteen years old, I was in a car accident that should have sent me through the windshield. A woman pulled in front of me, and my car hit the side of her car going forty miles per hour. I was not wearing a seatbelt, yet I felt something hold me in place. Everything in my car was thrown into or under the dash, except me.

I cannot explain by the laws of physics how that happened, but I believe God held me in place in that seat. Most people die in accidents such as that one. Did God love me more than someone else who did not survive an accident—perhaps a loved one of yours? No, I do not believe that! I came to the conclusion that God must have spared me for some particular purpose. Was it so that I could have two girls who somehow are critical to God's plans? Was it so that I could become a pastor and start a church? I simply do not know. Whatever it is, I very well may have already accomplished it, which is why I now wear my seatbelt everywhere I go! You see, I do not count on the fact that the same kind of thing will ever happen again.

Based on my own life experience, the experiences of the many people I have walked beside throughout my years of ministry, and the testimony of the Scriptures, I believe that most of the time God does not keep bad things from happening to us in this life. As I've said, we live in an imperfect world marred by sin and sickness and natural disasters, and God allows us to experience the effects and consequences of these things. God does not promise that we will not walk through the valley of the shadow of death. However, God has promised that when we walk that path, God will be with us. God does not keep people from doing evil, but God has taught us what is evil and what is good and has called us to do what is right. God does not always prevent tragedies from happening, but God works through them in ways we can see only in hindsight.

Romans 8:28 tells us that God works all things for good for those who love God. In other words, God does not cause bad things to happen, but when they do happen, God uses them to work for our good. God turns tragedy into triumph.

## Balancing Belief and Mystery

When it comes to the problem of suffering and divine providence—how God works in the world—there are a few things of which I am confident and many things that remain a mystery—and always will. The things of which I am confident are my beliefs. Again, I encourage you to wrestle with your own assumptions until you are confident of what you believe and why, allowing plenty of room for mystery.

To summarize, these are the things I believe about how God works in the world:

I believe that God is sovereign—the highest authority, king of the universe—yet God chooses to work in the world in certain ways.

I believe that God is involved in the affairs of the world but that God does not orchestrate every single circumstance. There is great mystery in this, to be sure.

The Scriptures testify that God has given us free will; therefore, I do not believe that everything is predetermined by God.

The Scriptures also affirm that God is just, loving, and kind and tell us that God will not do what is contrary to God's nature. Evil and sin are not from God. Therefore, I do not believe that God ordains or wills everything that happens.

I believe that although God does not cause pain and suffering and tragedy, God redeems it by working it for our good.

Beyond these things, I am content to trust God with the rest. I am content to pray to God for miracles and not be devastated when things do not happen as I had hoped. I am content in knowing that occasionally God breaks into our world for purposes I do not fully understand, but that most of the time the world operates according to the laws that govern it, which God established. I am content in knowing that there is much I do not know and cannot understand. I am content with mystery.

## MYSTERY AND THE BOOK OF JOB

The mystery of God's involvement in the world leads us to the Book of Job, which has as its focus the problem of suffering. Job is an epic poem. I believe, as many biblical scholars do, that it is a parable meant to teach an overarching point. Simply put, it is meant to challenge the assumption that you get what you deserve in life.

Most people in Job's day believed that if you did good, God would bless you, and if you did evil, God would punish you. This idea is still prevalent today. Often, in fact, life does seem to work this way. I often visualize life as a river or stream. When you are doing God's will, you are flowing with the current of God's will. Life seems to go better when you are flowing with that current. If you decide you no longer want to do God's will and you try to swim upstream against the current, you become exhausted. Sometimes you drown. There are consequences to going against the current that God has planned for humankind. However, the idea that you are being punished every time something bad happens is rightly questioned in the Scriptures. Some of the biblical authors affirmed the idea while others questioned it, including the author of Job.

The story begins this way: "There was once a man in the land of Uz whose name was Job. That man was blameless and upright, one who feared God and turned away from evil" (Job 1:1). Satan goes to God and tells God that Job is only righteous because God has blessed him. So God gives Satan permission to test Job by bringing bad to him. Job's crops and livestock are taken from him, and his children are killed in a terrible storm. In short order, Job is afflicted with a terrible disease so that he is in great pain with open sores upon his body.

## What Did Jesus Say?

Jesus spoke against the idea that suffering is God's punishment for sin:

*As he walked along, he saw a man blind from birth. His disciples asked him, "Rabbi, who sinned, this man or his parents, that he was born blind?" Jesus answered, "Neither this man nor his parents sinned; he was born blind so that God's works might be revealed in him."*

(John 9:1-3)

Some have missed the point and have decided that every bad thing that happens in life is from the devil. That is not what the Book of Job is meant to teach us. Rather, we are to note that God did not send these tragedies, and that Job is a righteous man who is suffering. His suffering, therefore, is not a punishment from God.

Job has three friends who come to him, and they get it right at first.

Now when Job's three friends heard of all these troubles that had come upon him, each of them set out from his home—Eliphaz the Temanite, Bildad the Shuhite, and Zophar the Naamathite. They met together to go and console and comfort him. When they saw him from a distance, they did not recognize him, and they raised their voices and wept aloud; they tore their robes and threw dust in the air upon their heads. They sat with him on the ground seven days and seven nights, and no one spoke a word to him, for they saw that his suffering was very great. (Job 2:11-13)

Here his friends do what friends should do when bad things happen. They simply sit in silence with him. They do not try to explain anything. They do not think that something they might say is going to make things better. They do not presume to have all the answers. They simply sit with him in silence and grieve with him.

Then, on the eighth day, Job begins to express all the feelings anyone would have after losing children and being afflicted with sores. *Why has this happened to me? I'm a good person. Why did God do this this? It's not right. It's not fair.*

By the way, it's important to give people room to say these things. They may be highly emotional and may not be thinking clearly, but they need to be able to express their feelings.

At this point Job's friends make the mistake of opening their mouths. Eliphaz, Bildad, and Zophar begin to lecture him. They tell him that because God is just, Job must have done something to deserve all of this. For the next 33 chapters, Job argues with his friends, who are joined by a fourth friend, Elihu. They continue to try to convince Job that he is being punished and must repent. He continues to assert his innocence and, in the process, God's injustice.

Finally, in chapter 38, God has heard enough and speaks directly to Job. His answer is both beautiful and unsatisfying. The poet writing this book describes nature—the stars, the depths of the sea, the wild animals, and the sea creatures. God watches over them all. Life happens day in and day out. And all of this is possible because God created all things and sustains them.

God does not explain suffering. Instead, God describes life and reasserts that God is the creator of it all. Job finally says this: "I spoke of things I did not understand, / things too wonderful for me to know" (Job 42:3, NIV). In the end Job humbles himself before God. The book concludes with God chastising Job's friends, saying that they had "not spoken of [God] what is right" (Job 42:7). Then God blesses Job, and there is joy in his life after his pain.

Such is the way of life. Some things we understand, and some things we do not. Nevertheless, God is just, loving, and merciful. We need to be very careful about attributing to God things that are not God's doing. We do not always have all the answers, and often our misguided responses bring pain rather than comfort to those who are suffering—just as in the story of Job.

Job lamented his friends' answers, saying:

> . . . miserable comforters are you all!
> Will your long-winded speeches never end?
>     What ails you that you keep on arguing?
> I also could speak like you,
>     if you were in my place;
> I could make fine speeches against you
>     and shake my head at you.
> But my mouth would encourage you;
>     comfort from my lips would bring you relief.
>                     (16:2-5, NIV)

Job needed encouragement and comfort, but his friends failed him. We can learn from their example. As Christians, we get it right when we listen, love, comfort, and show compassion to others in their time of need.

## THE RIGHT RESPONSE

Some time ago I received an e-mail from a church member whose husband, Jerry, was in the hospital fighting for his life in a battle against cancer—a battle he has since won. Her words convey an important message for all of us:

> I realize that you are writing about when Christians get it wrong, but I just wanted to make sure that people know what it looks like when Christians get it right. When they get it right, they send prayers through e-mail; they send silly cards and letters to the hospital to cheer you up; they move into your home and care for your children; they bring meals to you; they take your child to the emergency room at midnight; they help you assemble a Christmas gift for your children at 10 P.M. because they know you can't do it; they travel over 1,000 miles to hold your hand when you are alone and waiting with uncertainty; they give you gift cards for gas and food; they offer to be with your dying mother until you can get there; they buy you a tree to plant in her memory after she passes; and they give you hope, courage, and strength when you can't seem to find it on your own. Jerry and I were blessed to have been touched by Christians who did it right. We can never repay all the people who were at our side. And they don't want us to. They did it out of love. They did it because they were Christians, and that's what Christians do.

That is what the church looks like at its best—people filled with compassion who carry one another through the difficult times. The Latin word for compassion is *pati com,* which means to suffer with. We are to suffer with people, to stand by them.

The apostle Paul uses an interesting metaphor to speak of the church: the body of Christ. The idea is that God's primary vehicle for accomplishing God's purposes in our world is people. As the church, we are the physical incarnation of Jesus in the world. We are called to be his hands and feet and voice. When God wants to do something in the world, typically God does not intervene miraculously. Instead, God sends people to accomplish God's purposes. That is a daunting task, and one that we fail at often. But there are a lot of times when we do get it right. Regardless of the circumstances, we always get it right when we hold firmly to the hope we have in God and share that hope with others.

One day I attended a church member's funeral. She was a remarkable and vivacious young woman of thirty-one who had died of cancer. She had been clear in her living that cancer would not have the final word in her life. I spoke briefly with her father before the funeral began. Two days later, I was sitting with another father whose daughter had been missing for one week. In both instances, I imagined what I would be feeling if it were my daughter who had died of cancer or had been missing for a week. In the midst of these tragedies, the only thing these two fathers and their families had to hold onto is the hope that there really is a loving God who welcomed one daughter home and held firmly onto another daughter, wherever she was and whatever happened to her, and would never let go.

When some people experience tragedy, they turn away from God. But when they do this, all they have left is the tragedy. They are eliminating all hope. Faith in God is what gives us hope. Knowing that God loves us and that nothing can separate us from God's love (Romans 8:35-39) sustains us through the dark and difficult times.

When bad things happen, the right response is to carefully consider how God works in the world, let go of our anger, and embrace God's love. It is as simple as saying, "I need you, God, and I trust you." Then, in time, God is able to use us to minister to others who are hurting, bringing them compassion, comfort, courage, and hope in their time of need. This is the right response when bad things happen. And when we get it right, others are drawn to the love and hope of God through us.

# 5

# IN DEALING WITH HOMOSEXUALITY

*Then [Peter] heard a voice saying, "Get up, Peter; kill and eat." But [he] said, "By no means, Lord; for I have never eaten anything that is profane or unclean." The voice said to him again, a second time, "What God has made clean, you must not call profane."* . . . *And as [Peter] talked with [Cornelius], he went in and found that many had assembled; and he said to them, "You yourselves know that it is unlawful for a Jew to associate with or to visit a Gentile; but God has shown me that I should not call anyone profane or unclean."*

*(Acts 10:13-15, 27-28)*

As we begin this chapter I want to remind you that the focus of this book is the feelings and perceptions of young adults who have rejected the Christian faith concerning Christians. A 2010 Pew Forum study surveying various generations on religion and public life found that 26% of those born after 1981 reported no religious affiliation at all—twice the number of Baby Boomers who report no af-filiation. While many young people claim a religious affil-iation, only 18% report regularly attending worship (compared with 26% of Baby Boomers when they were this age). The Barna Group reports that 40% of young adults are "outsiders" to faith, and they substantiate the Pew findings, noting that young adults are increasingly secular. In describing some of the things that have turned them away from Christianity, I also hope to speak to those of us who are Christians, to help us think differently about how to be Christian. Jesus was a compelling figure who drew people to himself. Unfortunately, today's Christians often seem to repel young adults from the Christ they claim to serve.

I remind you, the reader, of this because we now wade into the most divisive issue in the church today, and one where there are huge generation differences—the issue of homosexuality. The 2007 Barna study, released as the book *unChristian*, found that 91% of young adults labeled Christianity "anti-homosexual," and this perception led many young adults to turn away from the church. This is how David Kinnaman, President of the Barna Group, characterized their findings:

> The most common perception of Christians today is that we're anti-homosexual. . . . They actually say that we show special contempt towards people who are gays and lesbians—that we don't have the ability to love these individuals. And when we interviewed young non-Christians, this was the same kind of sen-timent that they would say—"You've made it so easy to talk about this sin in black and white terms. . . . You have essentially lost the ability to love homo-sexuals in the way Jesus would do." . . . Here is a gen-eration who is not willing to be separated from sinful

people. They want to do what Jesus did and to get into peoples' lives and figure out what makes them tick—figure out where they are broken. They're not offended by sin. So when they see a group of people who are sort of separating from that—who say, well, no, we won't hang out with the prostitutes and sinners and the homosexuals—they criticize that group. They, rightly so, say they're unchristian—they're not like Jesus would do or be.

Here's what we don't need to miss: young adults who are outside the church are criticizing those of us who are inside the church for not being more like Jesus in how we interact with, talk to, and talk about homosexuals. Our treatment of homosexuals has become one of the primary reasons young adults are turning away from the church.

The 2010 Pew Forum study demonstrated what we have known for some time: young adults see this issue very differently from those who came before them. Of those born after 1981, 63% felt that homosexuality should be accepted by society, while only 35% of those over 65 years of age believed the same. Even among "evangelicals," 39% of young adults indicated that homosexuality should be accepted. When asked in the same survey if homosexual relations are always wrong, 78% of Baby Boomers said yes (down from a high of 88% among this generation twenty years ago). Forty-three percent of young adults said homosexual relations are always wrong.

I am not suggesting that Christians should determine morality by survey. I am suggesting that young adults see this issue differently than their parents and grandparents do. For young people, this issue is about excluding and hurting people they know and care about. They are also much more likely to see homosexuality, not as a willful decision to act in sinful, immoral, or perverted ways, but as a natural way that a small percentage of the population is either biologically or psychological "wired." They do not consider it offensive, immoral, or sinful when two people of the same sex love each other deeply.

Mainline churches are terribly divided over this issue. I predict that in ten to fifteen years evangelical churches will also be divided over this issue. And in twenty to twenty-five years, churches that continue to speak about homosexuality in the ways that many churches do today will have lost the larger part of a generation. The trends toward greater acceptance are not going to reverse, and that this will lead many people who are currently conservative on this issue to see it differently. I believe those in mainline churches who are currently leaving their denominations over this issue will find themselves in an interesting, isolated position twenty years from now.

It is important to recognize how serious of an issue this is for both sides in the divide. For "traditionalists"— Christians who support the traditional views that sexual intimacy and marriage are morally appropriate only when between a man and a woman—the issue is not only about homosexuality but also about the authority and role of Scripture in the life of Christians. Some Christians who are conservative on this issue are great advocates for social justice in other areas of life. Many are compassionate and welcome homosexuals into their churches. Where they struggle is the idea that the Bible presents a handful of clear prohibitions against homosexual sexual intercourse and, further, offers a significant number of Scriptures pointing toward God's plan for human intimacy being the complementary relationship between a man and a woman.

It is difficult for these persons to see how one can set aside these Scriptures and still maintain that the Bible has authority to speak in other areas of our lives. Why, they might ask, should we take seriously the Scriptures on helping the poor, or tithing, or loving our enemies when we have set aside Scriptures indicating that God's will is for marriage to be between a man and a woman? A great battle rages within the most compassionate of these persons between the desire to show compassion and fairness toward homosexuals and their belief that the Bible is "useful for teaching, for reproof, for correction, and for training in righteousness" (2 Timothy 3:16).

I recently had an exchange with a man on Facebook who spoke of "homophobes" and "co-dependent" preachers who were unwilling to speak the "truth." He was referring to traditionalists, but I think he did not understand the issue from the perspective of those he opposed. The use of terms such as "homophobe" is not helpful in persuading others, either—it inspires only defensiveness and anger.

On the other side, there clearly are people in the church who are insensitive, homophobic, and whose agenda on this issue is far less about pleasing God than it is about power and control. In an attempt to maintain a code of moral holiness in the church, they sometimes speak and act in ways that do not reflect the most important component of holiness: love.

Clearly, this is a hugely divisive issue because it pits values that Christians on both sides of the issue hold dear against one another. Several years ago I wrote a book, *Confronting the Controversies*, in which I laid out the Scriptural and pastoral arguments on both sides of this debate. Rather than rehash those arguments, I'd like to focus on two things that have been key in how I see this issue. The first is the nature of Scripture, and the second is a principle that guided Jesus' life—the principle that put people before rules.

## THE NATURE OF SCRIPTURE

I am increasingly convinced that when it comes to the debate over homosexuality within the Christian faith, the real underlying issue is not homosexuality but the nature of Scripture and its authority for our lives. Some people cannot see how we can set aside the handful of Scriptures that teach that same-sex intimacy is wrong without setting aside the whole of Scripture. It's unsettling to say that a particular moral teaching in the Scripture is no longer applicable to us. On what basis might we set aside these verses yet still maintain that the Bible is authoritative when it calls us to care for the poor, to love our enemies, and to do justice?

When I first became a Christian, my view of the Bible was fairly simplistic: Scripture is the Word of God. All Scripture was on an equal plane, and every word was chosen by God. It was inerrant and infallible (without mistake and completely flawless). I was taught the slogan, "The Bible says it; I believe it; that settles it."

Having read the Bible now virtually every day for thirty years, preaching it every weekend for nineteen years, and studying it in small groups and in pursuing my own study, I am aware that the Bible is more complicated than the simplistic slogans. We don't simply follow each word and apply it literally in our lives. Allow me to illustrate.

Most Christians eat pork, crab, shrimp, and, if they can afford it, lobster—all of which were forbidden by God in the Bible. We take our sabbath rest and day of worship on the first day of the week—Sunday—rather than on Saturday when God commanded the Israelites to observe the sabbath (Genesis 2:2-3), and we think nothing of mowing the yard or cleaning the house on our day off. Though Paul commands that "women should be silent in the churches" (1 Corinthians 14:34), many denominations, even fundamentalist churches, now allow women to speak in worship. When Jesus tells us to cut off our hands if they cause us to sin (see Matthew 5:30; Mark 9:43)—we don't take him literally; we *interpret* his words. Jesus tells us not to store up treasures on earth (see Matthew 6:19-21), yet most of us have retirement accounts. Is this not a violation of the actual words of Jesus?

Peter said to women, "Do not adorn yourselves outwardly by braiding your hair, and by wearing gold ornaments or fine clothing" (1 Peter 3:3); and Paul made a similar statement in his first letter to Timothy: "Women should dress themselves modestly and decently in suitable clothing, not with their hair braided, or with gold, pearls, or expensive clothes" (2:9). Despite these clear instructions from the Bible, many Christians don't take these teachings literally.

Beyond these things, we have passages in the Bible attributing to God things that seem wholly out of character with the way Jesus portrays God. The Bible commands the community to stone to death children who are disrespectful to their parents (see Deuteronomy 21:18-21). Those who work on the sabbath are also to be put to death (Exodus 31:12-15). If a priest's daughter becomes a prostitute, he is to burn her to death (Leviticus 21:9). How do we reconcile that with Jesus, who was a friend to prostitutes? And when God, in 1 Samuel 15:3, asks Saul to lead the armies of Israel against the Amalekites saying, "Now go and attack Amalek, and utterly destroy all that they have; do not spare them, but kill both man and woman, child and infant, ox and sheep, camel and donkey," is this really right? Did God really command that Saul destroy the Amalekites? Because 375 years earlier their ancestors had treated the Israelites with disrespect? Contrast this view of God with that portrayed in Luke 23:34, where Jesus (God the Son) hangs on the cross, looks upon the Romans and the Pharisees who crucified him, and prays, "Father, forgive them, for they know not what they are doing"? Is God vindictive, destroying a people 375 years after an offense, or is God one who shows mercy even to the people who torture, humiliate, and hang him on a cross?

Here's the question I ask concerning the very different pictures of God painted in 1 Samuel 15 and Luke 23: Did God change, or did human understanding of God change?

Biblical scholars speak of an idea called "progressive revelation." This is the idea that the promptings of God's Spirit were understood in the light of the concepts, ideas, and presuppositions of the times in which the biblical authors lived. This is important—Christians speak of the Bible as the "Word of God" but it was not dictated by God. Rather, it was written by people who were reflecting upon God, God's will, and God's promptings in their hearts. The authors were speaking to the people of their times, addressing the issues, needs, and challenges. Unlike any words about God in the Scripture, Jesus is the pure and complete Word of God. Thus, we read all Scripture in the light of what Jesus said and did.

Let's consider one of the most important examples of when a Christian leader came to understand that a particular teaching of Scripture was not God's timeless word, but instead it was time to set this teaching aside as no longer applicable.

Peter is a follower of Jesus, and a Jew. His Bible is the writings of the Old Testament. He is still striving to live according to its 613 laws. In the tenth chapter of Acts, Peter is in the town of Joppa on the southern edge of what is now Tel Aviv. He is hungry, and while his meal is being prepared, he is in prayer. As he prays, he enters into something like a trance. In that state, he sees a vision. A large sheet is let down in front of him by its four corners, and inside it are all kinds of animals—reptiles and birds that God clearly commands are not to be eaten (see Leviticus 11). God commanded them not to eat or even touch such animals. To touch them is to become defiled. Jews of that time could not eat pork, crab, lobster, shrimp, and a host of other things that God said were unclean. But look at Acts 10:11-15:

> [Peter] saw heaven opened and something like a large sheet coming down, being lowered to the ground by its four corners. In it were all kinds of four-footed creatures and reptiles and birds of the air. Then he heard a voice saying, "Get up, Peter; kill and eat." But Peter said, "By no means, Lord; for I have never eaten anything that is profane or unclean." The voice said to him again, a second time, "What God has made clean, you must not call profane."

Peter has a vision in which he hears God telling him to do something that the Bible had expressly forbidden. Here, 1,200 years after the time the Law was given, God says to Peter, "Do not call anything unclean that I have made clean." This passage is the beginning of something huge that God is doing.

While Peter is trying to make sense of his vision, there's a knock at the door. Three Gentiles (non-Jews) have been sent by a Roman commander named Cornelius to fetch Peter. Peter goes with them to Cornelius' home. A good Jew would not have entered, because Gentiles were considered unclean. But Peter has an epiphany, he suddenly understands—The rules are changing! Listen to how he explains his epiphany to this house full of Gentiles: "You yourselves know that it is unlawful for a Jew to associate with or to visit a Gentile; but God has shown me that I should not call anyone profane or unclean" (Acts 10:28).

Peter's world is changing, he must move beyond a mindset that says, "The Bible says it; I believe it; that settles it." Instead he says, *"The Bible says it, but I think God is up to something new, so I will listen to and follow God."*

None of this sets aside the Bible's teaching on homosexuality, but it does give us permission to ask questions such as these: "When Leviticus 18:22 and 20:13 teach that same-sex intimacy is an abomination and, in 20:13, that those who participate in it should be put to death, does this capture the heart, character, and eternal will of God, or do these verses capture the values and reflections of a people who lived 3,200 years ago and who had little understanding of homosexuality?" Does God really want us to put to death homosexuals? And when Paul speaks in Romans 1:26-27 about women and men committing shameless acts with one another by giving up the "natural" form of sexual intimacy for the unnatural, was God speaking and declaring homosexuality to be shameless and unnatural, or was Paul describing first century Jewish understandings of what was natural and unnatural?

Now you might rightly ask, "If we start setting aside certain Scriptures, where do we stop?" That's a great question, and an important one. Do we set aside every Scripture we don't like and find a rationalization for setting it aside? No, but we do engage in serious study and reflection when we are faced with serious issues, and we don't simply quote a verse or two and consider the matter settled.

John Wesley, the founder of Methodism, is said to have understood that Scripture is the primary basis for our faith and practice. It contains all that is necessary for our salvation. But he also believed that to rightly interpret and apply Scripture in life, we need the benefit of the church's theological, ethical, and biblical reflections over the last 2,000 years—including the work of scholars, commentators, ethicists, and theologians. He also believed that we bring to our reading of Scripture our rational minds and scientific knowledge. And finally, Wesley called us to bring our life experience and the witness of the Spirit to bear upon our study, interpretation, and application of Scripture in our lives.

You may think this is all so much rationalization—I do not. I see it as the essential work of rightly handling the Scriptures. This is this process that allowed us to conclude that though slavery is allowed in the Bible, it is inconsistent with the broader message of Scripture concerning the dignity of humankind and of justice. This process allows us to conclude that though the Bible speaks of women "keeping silent in the church," the dominant biblical themes speak to the shared dignity of men and women. Both were created in the image of God, and partnership rather than male dominance is more aligned with justice.

All of this leads me to be open to the possibility that God's perspective on homosexuality may be different from what is in Leviticus and in Paul's letter to the church at Rome. It may be that heterosexuality is God's ideal and intention for humanity; our bodies themselves bear witness to this, as does the Bible's teaching about God creating us male and female. But I have come to believe that God's compassion and understanding toward persons who do not fit these norms—whose fundamental wiring seems to be oriented towards same-sex attraction—are undoubtedly greater than the Scriptures would indicate. I find it difficult to believe that God—who is rich in mercy, who formed us in our mothers' wombs, and whose love is higher and deeper and wider than we can imagine—truly looks upon homosexuals as an abomination. The broader witness of Scripture points me towards God's compassion, mercy, kindness, and love.

## GOD'S LOVE OF PEOPLE

This understanding of the nature of Scripture opened the door for me to see this issue differently than I once had, but when I began to know and care about people who are homosexual, my heart truly changed. I pastor a congregation of 17,000 people. Assuming persons with same-sex attractions make up 5% of the population, there are likely 850 people in the congregation I serve who are homosexual. Add to this the number of people who have family members who are gay or lesbian, and the number increases significantly. One Sunday I asked members of our congregation to raise their hands if they had a family member, close friend, or someone they cared about who was homosexual. Nearly everyone raised his or her hand.

I think of Mary. I have been her pastor since she was two years old. She's a sweet, kind, and humble young woman who grew up in our children's program, participated in our youth program, and is now attending college. Mary recently told me she was homosexual. I cried as I read some of the things other Christians have said to her. I think of Aaron, who grew up in our youth group, who served on our church council, and who was quite serious about wanting to follow Jesus Christ. I think of Kristin, who I watched grow up. She is now a schoolteacher and in a covenant relationship with her partner.

Many of my questions about homosexuality are yet to be answered. There are dimensions of the discussion that don't fit neatly into the arguments of the Right or the Left. But this one thing I am certain of—I don't want be a church that turns away young adults like Mary, Aaron, or Kristin.

There are many things about Jesus that I love. One of them is that he put people before rules. He did this consistently. He had a heart for people whom others deemed sinful. He went out of his way to touch those who were unclean. And in him, they found hope and love. It was the Pharisees who were incensed that Jesus had fellowship with "sinners and tax collectors." Even the disciples were a bit surprised by some of the people Jesus associated with. For Jesus, people came before rules.

One of my favorite stories from Jesus' ministry is found in John 4, where Jesus waited for a woman at a well in Samaria. It speaks volumes about Jesus' character and heart toward people others might be tempted to shun. This woman had been married and divorced five times, and at this point, she was living with a man who was not her husband. This was quite scandalous in her day. Jesus

## What Did Jesus Say?

*So he came to a Samaritan city called Sychar near the plot of ground that Jacob had given to his son Joseph. Jacob's well was there, and Jesus, tired out by his journey, was sitting by the well. It was about noon. A Samaritan woman came to draw water, and Jesus said to her, "Give me a drink." (His disciples had gone to the city to buy food.) The Samaritan woman said to him, "How is it that you, a Jew, ask a drink of me, a woman of Samaria?" (Jews do not share things in common with Samaritans.) Jesus answered her, "If you knew the gift of God, and who it is that is saying to you, 'Give me a drink,' you would have asked him, and he would have given you living water." The woman said to him, "Sir, you have no bucket, and the well is deep. Where do you get that living water? Are you greater than our ancestor Jacob, who gave us the well, and with his sons and his flocks drank from it?" Jesus said to her, "Everyone who drinks of this water will be thirsty again, but those who drink of the water that I will give them will never be thirsty. The water that I will give will become in them a spring of water gushing up to eternal life." The woman said to him, "Sir, give me this water, so that I may never be thirsty or have to keep coming here to draw water." Jesus said to her, "Go, call your husband, and come back." The woman answered him, "I have no husband." Jesus said to her, "You are right in saying, 'I have no husband'; for you have had five husbands, and the one you have now is not your husband. What you have said is true!" The woman said to him, "Sir, I see that you are a prophet. . . . I know that Messiah is coming" (who is called Christ). "When he comes, he will proclaim all things to us." Jesus said to her, "I am he, the one who is speaking to you." Just then his disciples came. They were astonished that he was speaking with a woman, but no one said, "What do you want?" or, "Why are you speaking with her?" Then the woman left her water jar and went back to the city. She said to the people, "Come and see a man who told me everything I have ever done! He cannot be the Messiah, can he?" They left the city and were on their way to him. . . . Many Samaritans from that city believed in him because of the woman's testimony, "He told me everything I have ever done."*

(John 4:5-19, 25-30, 39)

spoke to her and offered her "living water" so that she would "never thirst again"—that is, the fullness of life in Christ, complete with the power of the Holy Spirit. Interestingly, he did not lecture her on the evils of divorce or cohabitation. He did not even say, "Go leave the man you are living with." At times Jesus did say, "Go and sin no more," but not here in this story. Does that mean that he was saying it's okay to live together outside of marriage? I don't think so. I think he was saying that there were more important things than this, and that people come before rules. He offered her grace. And in response, the woman became the first missionary and evangelist to the Samaritans, causing many in her city to believe in Jesus.

This leads me to an e-mail I received a couple of years ago that describes what I think it looks like when Christians get it right regarding homosexuality.

> I am a lesbian who has a partner and three children. I have never been to your church. But this e-mail is not about being gay or about the church's stance on being gay. It is about one of your members whose name is Carol. Carol lives next door to me. She was one of the first neighbors to come and say "hello." She was warm and inviting, and one day she invited us to church. . . . I told her I was gay, and she didn't raise an eyebrow or frown. I told her my father was a Southern Baptist preacher and I hold very strong beliefs. When a church shuns me, it hurts more than words can express. She invited me again to church. I checked out your church's website and was impressed that the church was talking about this issue and not just praying it would go away.
>
> I have never valued a church by the number of people in the pews or the amount of money in the offering. What I am moved by is a woman so touched by

your church that she came into my heart. She lives a life that so many could learn from. She opens up her home to people in need. She checks on those who aren't feeling well. And she shared Christ with a woman she knew was gay because it was in her heart to do it. I have been truly blessed by this woman, and I am hoping to visit your church in the future.

Not all Christians see the issue of homosexuality in the same way. The church is divided on this issue. But even in a divided church, we can agree that we wish to be the kind of church in which men and women who are gay and lesbian find the warmth and welcome and love of Jesus Christ.

I think Christians get it wrong when we speak in ways that bring harm and alienation to God's gay children; I think we get it right when, even in our uncertainty, we express the love and welcome of the One who offered living water to the woman at the well.

# 6

# WHEN CHRISTIANS GET IT RIGHT

*"Beloved, since God loved us so much, we also ought to love one another. No one has ever seen God; if we love one another, God lives in us, and his love is perfected in us. . . . So we have known and believe the love that God has for us. God is love, and those who abide in love abide in God, and God abides in them. . . . We love because he first loved us. Those who say, 'I love God,' and hate their brothers or sisters, are liars; for those who do not love a brother or sister whom they have seen, cannot love God whom they have not seen. The commandment we have from him is this: those who love God must love their brothers and sisters also."*

*(1 John 4:11-12, 16, 19-21)*

Christians have always struggled to "get it right." Most of the New Testament was written to address Christians who were "getting it wrong." They struggled with self-righteousness, hypocrisy, judgmentalism, spiritual pride, moral compromise, and a host of other issues. The New Testament letters were often aimed at correcting these things.

Underlying all of the other counsel the apostles gave for how Christians can get it right is one common refrain: To get it right is to love. Peter says it this way, "Love covers a multitude of sins" (1 Peter 4:8). James writes, "You do well if you really fulfill the royal law according to the scripture, 'You shall love your neighbor as yourself' " (James 2:8). John is even more bold in his first epistle, "Whoever does not love does not know God, for God is love" (1 John 4:8).

Among the most dysfunctional churches in the New Testament, where Christians were getting it wrong, was the church at Corinth in Greece. Their church was fractured and filled with Christians who acted in ways that scarcely resembled the Christ they claimed to follow. To these Christians Paul wrote very directly, saying,

> If I speak in the tongues of mortals and of angels, but do not have love, I am a noisy gong or a clanging cymbal. And if I have prophetic powers, and understand all mysteries and all knowledge, and if I have all faith, so as to remove mountains, but do not have love, I am nothing. (1 Corinthians 13:1-2)

Then he goes on to describe the love that Christians are to show:

> Love is patient; love is kind; love is not envious or boastful or arrogant or rude. It does not insist on its own way; it is not irritable or resentful; it does not rejoice in wrongdoing, but rejoices in the truth. It bears all things, believes all things, hopes all things, endures all things. Love never ends. . . . And now faith, hope, and love abide, these three; and the greatest of these is love. (1 Corinthians 13:4-8a, 13)

Why does Paul place such strong emphasis on love? Because if you boiled down the gospel to one word, it would be *love*. Jesus commanded his disciples to love God with their entire being and to love their neighbors as they love themselves. Jesus goes on to tell his disciples that the world will know that they were his disciples by their love. They are to love one another, to love their neighbor, to love those in need, and even to love their enemies.

## What Did Jesus Say?

*"You shall love the Lord your God with all your heart, and with all your soul, and with all your strength, and with all your mind; and your neighbor as yourself."*
(Luke 10:27)

*"I give you a new commandment, that you love one another. Just as I have loved you, you also should love one another. By this everyone will know that you are my disciples, if you have love for one another."*
(John 13:34-35)

Even as I write these words, I realize how often I fall short of them. When we Christians get it wrong, it is because we have forgotten or neglected these basic teachings of Jesus. But when we get it right, we love as Jesus loved. We practice sacrificial love. And that is a powerful witness. It has the capacity to change the world.

Let's take a closer look at the two great commandments Jesus gave us, instructing us to love God and neighbor.

## THE SHEMA AND THE JESUS CREED

"You shall love the Lord your God with all your heart, and with all your soul, and with all your mind.' This is the greatest and first commandment. And a second is like it: 'You shall love your neighbor as yourself' " (Matthew 22:37-39). These are known as the two great commandments for Christians. The first of these great commandments was familiar to every faithful Jew. They called it the *Shema*, and they memorized it and recited it often (see Deuteronomy 6:4-9). Jesus added the word *mind*, inviting us to engage our mind as well as our hearts, souls, and strength in service to God.

This first commandment points to a fundamental assertion of the Christian and Jewish faiths: There is one God, and God created humankind for relationship with God. God loves us, and because God created and sustains us in love, God is worthy of our love. We are only fully human when we are in relationship with God.

## What Did Jesus Say?

*"Give to everyone who begs from you; and if anyone takes away your goods, do not ask for them again. Do to others as you would have them do to you."*
(Luke 6:30-31)

*"Love your enemies, do good to those who hate you, bless those who curse you, pray for those who abuse you."*
(Luke 6:27-28)

*"No one has greater love than this, to lay down one's life for one's friends."*
(John 15:13)

Then Jesus added something to the Shema—the command from Leviticus 19:18: "You shall love your neighbor as yourself." Jesus actually modified one of the most important creeds or acts of worship of the Jewish faith. Professor Scott McKnight, who has written a book on the two great commandments, refers to them as "the Jesus Creed." He notes that adding this line would be tantamount to you or I adding a line to the Apostle's or Nicene Creed.[9] But, of course, Jesus had the authority to do it. The idea conveyed in the second commandment is still thoroughly Jewish, and it truly does summarize the entire Law and Prophets as Jesus said. Still, by elevating it to this place, Jesus made it clear that we cannot love God if we do not love our neighbor. These two go hand in hand.

John Wesley, Methodism's founder, said it this way, "There is no holiness without social holiness," meaning that you cannot pursue holiness if you are not engaged in loving your neighbor. Wesley rightly noted that the goal of the Christian life is summed up by the two great commandments. If we are growing as Christians, we will be ever deepening our love for God and ever growing in our love for others.

This is precisely what the apostle John said in his epistle when he told us to love because God loved us first. Then he said, "Those who say, 'I love God,' and hate their brothers or sisters, are liars; for those who do not love a brother or sister whom they have seen, cannot love God whom they have not seen" (1 John 4:20). We love others because God loves us, and we cannot claim to fulfill the great command to love God if we are not also loving our neighbor.

Moses commanded the Israelites to recite the great command, the Shema, every morning as they awoke and every evening as they went to bed so that they would remember the love of God and their mission of reciprocating God's love. Professor McKnight suggests that we Christians might want to use the Jesus Creed as our Jewish friends use the Shema. Perhaps we should recite the two great commandments every morning and every evening in prayer. After reading his suggestion, I've included this practice in my own morning and evening prayers, saying, "Lord, help me to love you with all my heart, soul, mind, and strength. And help me, in every way, in every inter-action, with everyone, to express your love." Then in the evening as I prepare for bed, I pray, "God, forgive me for failing to perfectly love you and others. Even as I sleep, form my soul to more truly love you and others." Think about what could happen if we made that our prayer every single day, morning and night.

## LOVE AS THE CENTRAL CHRISTIAN ETHIC

These two great commands to love—to love God and to love neighbor—define Christian ethics. When we are unsure of what the right thing to do is, we simply need to ask ourselves this question: In this situation, what is the most loving thing I can do? Typically the answer will come quickly.

### What Did Jesus Say?

*[A man] asked Jesus, "And who is my neighbor?" Jesus replied, "A man was going down from Jerusalem to Jericho, and fell into the hands of robbers, who stripped him, beat him, and went away, leaving him half dead. Now by chance a priest was going down that road; and when he saw him, he passed by on the other side. So likewise a Levite, when he came to the place and saw him, passed by on the other side. But a Samaritan while traveling came near him; and when he saw him, he was moved with pity. He went to him and bandaged his wounds, having poured oil and wine on them. Then he put him on his own animal, brought him to an inn, and took care of him. The next day he took out two denarii, gave them to the innkeeper, and said, 'Take care of him; and when I come back, I will repay you whatever more you spend.' Which of these three, do you think, was a neighbor to the man who fell into the hands of the robbers?" He said, "The one who showed him mercy." Jesus said to him, "Go and do likewise."* (Luke 10:29-37)

This question also helps to point us toward the kind of love Jesus was talking about. It is not some sappy, romantic, or feel-good kind of love. The kind of love he was referring to was not a feeling but a way of looking, thinking about, and acting toward others that involves seeking their best, putting their needs before your own, and practicing kindness toward them at some personal cost—even when that kindness is undeserved. Jesus himself defined what this love looks like on multiple occasions. He told us to love our enemies. Clearly this is not a feeling but a way of acting toward them that seeks their good even though they don't deserve it. He told us that the greatest example of this love is actually laying down one's life for another. He then lay down his own life for humankind through his suffering and death on the cross.

He also gave us a parable aimed at teaching us what this kind of love looks like—the parable of the good Samaritan. Jesus has been talking about the commandment to love one's neighbor as oneself, and a lawyer spoke up and asked, "But who is my neighbor?" His question was really, "Who do I not have to love?" To answer him, Jesus told the story of a Jewish man who was going from Jerusalem to Jericho—a 16-mile journey that would take, on foot, about 6 ½ hours. On the way he was accosted by thieves who stole his donkey (if he had one), his clothing, and his money. They beat him and left him for dead.

Two religious leaders came along on the road, saw the man, and walked by on the other side. Why? They had forgotten the basics. Perhaps they were focused on their rules—stopping to help would involve violating rules that said you couldn't even let your shadow fall on a dead person without becoming ceremonially unclean. Or maybe they were focused on their schedules—stopping to help would mean rescheduling everything for the next week if they became unclean. Or they might have been concerned about their pocketbooks—stopping to help would require actually providing assistance for the man—or the risks involved—stopping to help would mean that they, too, might be beaten and robbed. Or perhaps they realized that if they picked up this man, he would have to ride on the donkey and they would have to walk 16 miles. Whatever the reason, both passed by, assuming someone else would help.

Then a third man came along. This man was an unlikely hero in the story because he was a Samaritan. Jews had a particular disdain for Samaritans in Jesus' day. They were considered heretics and traitors. But this man saw the Jew lying on the side of the road, and he felt pity. He stopped to help him, bandaged his wounds, put him on his donkey, cared for him, and left $1,000 to be used by the innkeeper to continue to care for the man. This man illustrated what Jesus meant by love.

Love is willing to be inconvenienced, to take risks, and to do what is right and kind and caring even to those who don't deserve it. This is what Jesus calls us, his followers, to do. Jesus is raising us up to change the world by doing the hard work of loving others. And in the process, we will be tearing down walls of hate and healing the brokenness in the world.

The parable of the good Samaritan is what Dr. Martin Luther King, Jr., preached on the night before he was assassinated. He was in Memphis, Tennessee, marching for better pay for both white and black sanitation workers. King noted that the first two men asked the wrong question. They looked at the man left for dead and asked, "What will happen to me if I stop to help?" But the Samaritan asked the question that love dictates: "What will happen to him if I don't stop to help?" Love puts the needs of the other before oneself. When we forget this, we focus on some matter of dogma or some particular behavior in others that we find sinful, or we demonize those who see the world differently than we do, or we adopt a faith that is all about ourselves. When we forget the central Christian ethic of love, we get it wrong.

## GETTING IT RIGHT

Of course, we Christians do not have a corner on the market when it comes to getting it wrong. Every human being is afflicted with the tendency to get it wrong. We call this sin. The seven deadly sins—lust, gluttony, greed, indifference, hurting others, envy, and pride—are universal temptations, not unique to Christians. We all struggle with these temptations.

So, it should be no surprise that sometimes we Christians get it wrong. Christianity does not invite perfect people to join up. It invites people who are prone to get it wrong, and it offers them grace. As one person told me, "If I never got it wrong, I would not need Christianity!" Christianity is about forgiveness, not perfection.

Still, it's important for us to remember that the Christian life—the life of discipleship—does not stop at forgiveness. The aim of the Christian life is to get it right. Theologians call this aim "sanctification"—being made holy. And holiness looks like love. If we are being made holy and are growing in our faith, over time we should become more loving, not less so. When we find people who have been Christians for some time, the proof that they are maturing in the faith is not how much of the Bible they have memorized, or how systematic their theology is, or even how well they avoid the more obvious sins.

The proof of spiritual growth is found in the practice of love.

When we get it right as Christians, we become a living witness of the love of God. When we actually love, we find it impossible to be closed-minded, judgmental, hypocritical, insensitive, or anti-homosexual. And this kind of love is utterly compelling, even for people who are not sure what they think of Christianity. In fact, the most compelling argument for Christianity is a Christian who demonstrates the love of God selflessly to another.

As a pastor, I have had the joy of watching many Christians working to get it right. Having acknowledged some of the ways Christians get it wrong throughout this book, I'd like to tell you about some of the ways they get it right.

Some time ago Vincent began attending our church. He's a gifted vocalist in his thirties who sang heavy metal and classic rock for years. Vincent is also afflicted with Tourette's syndrome. His form of Tourette's is known as *coprolalia*, and includes the spontaneous utterance of words that most people suppress—swear words. Vincent was diagnosed when he was an adolescent. From that time on he had felt unwelcome in church. We have a large sanctuary, but it was easy to tell when Vincent was present, starting with his first visit. As I was preaching, he would blurt out swear words. It was a little unnerving at first. Some with children who did not understand what was happening moved to another part of the sanctuary. But almost instantly some people realized that Vincent had Tourette's. When Vincent would show up for worship, a group of people sat near him and reassured him it was okay. Vincent thought that perhaps it would help if people knew his story, so one weekend we told his story and then invited him to sing. When he was finished singing about his life, the congregation rose to their feet in a standing ovation that lasted for several minutes. What they were saying to Vincent was, "We love you. We want you here. You are a gift from God!"

As they stood applauding, I saw the church as it is meant to be, a community of people who welcome others with genuine love. They got it right. '

Chris and his wife, Tammi, a remarkable young couple I know, moved from the suburbs to a crime-ridden neighborhood in Kansas City. Drive-by shootings, sexual assault, and drug houses are nearly a daily part of life in their community. But they felt called to move there in order to bring hope to children and youth who live there. They started the Hope Center, which is seeking to transform the neighborhood and the children there. Today hundreds of people are finding hope through the education programs, medical clinic, and youth groups Chris and Tammi have launched. Chris and Tammi are Christians who get it right.

I have watched as people do the most giving and sacrificial things caring for one another in the church. Lori's church friends watched her children, mowed her yard, put together her children's Christmas presents on Christmas Eve, and flew one thousand miles to be with her at M.D. Anderson Cancer Center in Houston where her husband, Jerry, was in treatment for cancer. She told me she did not know how she could have made it without this care. That's what it looks like when Christians get it right.

There was Amy, who saw a young, pregnant teenager leaving McDonald's without a winter coat on a cold Kansas City evening. She ran to her car, got her own coat, and gave it to the girl, beginning a relationship with a teenage mother who needed a friend.

There was David, who saw a young man in a suit walking home from work in the rain. He stopped to give him a ride and discovered the young man walked two miles each way to work in the only suit he owned. The next morning David dropped off a bicycle and began a relationship with the young man that culminated in the young man receiving a scholarship to go to college.

Greg used the influence of his construction company to help break down racial barriers in Kansas City. Danielle and JT spent the first year of their married life in South Africa seeking to serve people in extreme poverty. Steve gives his employees paid leave for humanitarian service. Reed and Debi welcomed a young man into their home to help him have a future. Connie and Reid weekly devote time to supporting Aaron, a kid from the projects whom they love as if he were there own. Karla leads hundreds of church members to visit the forgotten people— the nursing home residents no one else ever visits at thirty area nursing homes. Hundreds of people in our church volunteer in our Matthew's Ministry, serving more than one hundred special-needs children, youth, and adults and providing respite for their parents. They give up their weeknights and weekends to throw parties, lead groups, and love our special-needs members. They are all Christians who get it right.

I could fill a lengthy book with stories like these. I'm not suggesting that only Christians do these things. I know there are others who do the same. But in my travels to Honduras and Haiti, to Zambia and South Africa, to the Gulf Coast after Hurricane Katrina and the inner city in Kansas City, nearly all of the people I have met doing humanitarian work are Christians. Christians often get it wrong, but tens of millions of quiet Christians daily seek, without fanfare or accolades, to get it right.

When Christians get it right, we share the love of God we have experienced through Jesus Christ—a love that is sacrificial, unconditional, filled with mercy, and ultimately life transforming. God's love compels us to want to be more loving. And the Holy Spirit and the disciplines of the Christian life are all aimed at helping us to know and live God's love.

So, if we want to get it right, we must continually ask ourselves this question: When people look at us, what do they learn about Christianity? What kind of witness do they see in us—as individuals and as the church?

In his letter to the Colossians, the apostle Paul speaks about what people see in us, and he describes this as our clothing:

> [Strip] off the old self, with its practices and [clothe] yourselves with the new self. . . . As God's chosen ones, holy and beloved, clothe yourselves with compassion, kindness, humility, meekness, and patience. . . . Above all, clothe yourselves with love. (3:9-14)

Throughout this book young adults have been teaching us that many of the Christians they've known have clothed themselves with hypocrisy, judgmentalism, narrow-mindedness, and worse. It's time to strip these things off and to clothe ourselves with love.

Today's young adults need to see us get it right. Let's be the kind of Christians who live the gospel of courageous, compassionate, sacrificial love. When they see us loving in this way, I believe they will want to come and see the gospel that inspires such acts.

# POSTSCRIPT

You may be wondering what happened with John, the young man I mentioned often throughout the book. After our initial conversation, I asked John if he would come back and allow me to interview him before a camera so that I could share his perspectives both with my own congregation and with a broader audience of church leaders. Later that year he attended worship with us—it was the first time he'd been in church in years. Sometime later he asked if I would officiate at his wedding. I was honored that he asked, and I had the joy of sitting down with John and Nancy in preparation for their wedding. I enjoyed celebrating their union. In preparing this book, I asked John to read it and give me his feedback.

Has John become a Christian? No, not yet. I sense an openness I did not see the first time we met. And though we don't get the chance to talk often, I believe he values our relationship as do I. My hope and prayer is that one day he will become a follower of Jesus Christ.

This book is dedicated to him.

# NOTES

1. See http://whoisthisjesus.googlepages.com/gandhiandchristianity.
2. Giorgio de Santillana, *The Crime of Galileo* (University of Chicago Press, 1978); p. 310.
3. Martin Luther King, Jr., *A Testament of Hope*, ed. James M. Washington (HarperSanFrancisco, 1986); p. 594.
4. One billion Catholics, 300 million Orthodox, and 300 million Mainline Protestants leaves 600 million Christians.
5. See http://www.tentmaker.org/tracts/Universalists.html, which includes Clement of Alexandria, Origen, Athanasius, Ambrose, John Chrysostom, Eusebius, Gregory of Nyssa, and Jerome among those who held the Universalist view.
6. Dan Kimball, *They Like Jesus but Not the Church* (Zondervan, 2007); p. 166.
7. Blog post "Katrina: God's Judgment on America" by David Crowe, available at http://www.beliefnet.com/News/2005/09/Katrina-Gods-Judgment-On-America.aspx.
8. Leslie D. Weatherhead, *The Will of God* (Abingdon, 1972); pp. 12–13.
9. Scott McKnight, *The Jesus Creed: Loving God, Loving Others* (Paraclete, 2004); p. 9.

*Pick up the original book.*

**CHRISTIANS WOULD RATHER JUDGE ME THAN GET TO KNOW ME**

...re and more young adults have opted out of Christianity and the church.
The reason? Christians.

# More Studies From Adam Hamilton

DVD and Leader's Guide available for each study

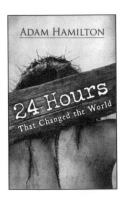

24 Hours That Changed
the World
ISBN: 9780687465552
$ 18.00

Seeing Gray in a World of
Black and White
ISBN: 9780687649693
$ 22.95

Christianity and World Religions
Participant's Book
ISBN: 9780687494309
$ 12.00

Confronting the Controversies
Participant's Book
ISBN: 9780687346004
$ 12.00